Ammochostos
(Famagusta) Bay

Salamis

**Ammochostos
(Famagusta /
Gazimağusa)**
Lala Mustafa Paşa Mosque

OUTHEAST

**Agia
Napa**

**Nissi
Beach**

**Potamos
Liopetriou**

*Cape Gkreko
(Capo Greko)*

ara
tle

Ka

TWINPACK
Cyprus

LARA DUNSTON

If you have any comments or suggestions for this guide you can contact the editor at
Twinpacks@theAA.com

AA Publishing
Find out more about AA Publishing and the wide range of services the AA provides by visiting our website at theAA.com/bookshop

How to Use This Book

KEY TO SYMBOLS

➕ Map reference

✉ Address

☎ Telephone number

🕐 Opening/closing times

🍴 Restaurant or café

🚌 Nearest bus route

⛴ Nearest ferry route

♿ Facilities for visitors with disabilities

❓ Other practical information

▷ Further information

ℹ Tourist information

✋ Admission charges: Expensive (over €9/17YTL), Moderate (€3–€9/6–17YTL), and Inexpensive (under €3/6YTL)

★ Major Sight   ★ Minor Sight

👣 Walks   🚌 Drives

🏬 Shops

🎵 Entertainment and Activities

🍴 Restaurants

This guide is divided into four sections

• Essential Cyprus: An introduction to the island and tips on making the most of your stay.

• Cyprus by Area: We've broken the island into five areas, and recommended the best sights, shops, restaurants, activities, entertainment and nightlife venues in each one. Suggested walks and drives help you to explore.

• Where to Stay: The best hotels, whether you're looking for luxury, budget or something in between.

• Need to Know: The info you need to make your trip run smoothly, including getting about by public transport, weather tips, emergency phone numbers and useful websites.

Navigation In the Cyprus by Area chapter, we've given each area its own colour, which is also used on the locator maps throughout the book and the map on the inside front cover.

Maps The fold-out map accompanying this book is a comprehensive map of Cyprus. The grid on this fold-out map is the same as the grid on the locator maps within the book. The grid references to these maps are shown with capital letters, for example A1. The grid references to the Lefkosia (Nicosia/Lefkoşa) town plan are shown with lower-case letters, for example a1.

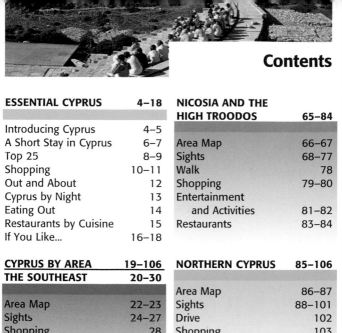

Contents

CONTENTS

Introducing Cyprus

The hottest of the Mediterranean islands has been attracting visitors for thousands of years. With a seemingly endless summer, agreeable food and wine, and easygoing locals, it's no wonder so many have decided to stay on seductive Cyprus.

As compelling as it is, Cyprus' delights don't end at the aquamarine waters lapping its pristine beaches. Packed with remnants of its history, Cyprus has hosted everyone from Romans to Egyptians, Ottomans to the British, and their lasting legacies have visitors fascinated by the connections.

In the Greek-speaking south, Larnaka (Larnaca), Limassol (Lemesos) and Pafos (Paphos), all have a breezy, easy-going feel more akin to small towns than bustling beach resorts. A myriad of resorts dotted around them cater for everyone, and while they're hard to leave, the delights of exploring Cyprus are hard to ignore.

The Troodos Mountains are spectacular, with winding roads cutting through thick forests, the scent of pine, and in winter, the curious lure of fresh powder snow in the Mediterranean. Whichever path you take, you'll discover remote monasteries, such as remarkable Kykkos, renowned for its icon paintings and mosaics. A trip to the romantic Rock of Aphrodite for sunset is a must, and for the more adventurous, a walk or drive to Lara for its desolate beaches.

Equally rewarding is visiting the Turkish-speaking north. Picturesque Kyrenia (Keryneia/Girne) harbour is photogenic, as are the breathtaking views down to it from Belapais Abbey. Famagusta (Ammochostos/ Gazimağusa) tempts visitors inside its Venetian walls, while Nicosia (Lefkosia/Lefkoşa) offers a fascinating view of life in a divided capital.

Archaeology buffs will already have circled sights such as the hilltop splendour of Kourion, Pafos mosaics, and the precariously perched St. Hilarion Castle, but there's no need to rush on laidback Cyprus. The locals won't mind. They know that many visitors not only come back every year, some never leave.

Facts + Figures

- Cyprus' population is 789,300 in the south, 264,172 in the north.
- Cyprus has over 2 million visitors a year; tourism provides employment for some 35,000 people.

MEDITERRANEAN DIET

It's true, the Mediterranean diet is one of the healthiest in the world. Fresh seasonal ingredients, local herbs and spices, a dash of fantastic olive oil—all taken while sitting in the sun sipping local wine on a brilliant afternoon—it's almost a crime that it's good for you!

GREEK? TURKISH?

While the south of Cyprus is seen as Greek, it's actually its own republic–the Republic of Cyprus (RoC). However, it is Greek speaking and essentially Greek in character. The Turkish-speaking north is the self-declared Turkish Republic of Northern Cyprus (TRNC), but this is only recognized by Turkey itself.

SUNSHINE GALORE

Cyprus in summer is a hot place, certainly the hottest of the Mediterranean islands, and, of course, sun worshippers love it. Cyprus has an average of 3,350 hours of sunshine a year and there is barely a drop of rain between May and October. It's hard to imagine that winter days can be cool with snow falling on the highest ground, creating a winter wonderland among the pine trees.

A Short Stay in Cyprus

DAY 1: NICOSIA

Morning Visit the **Cyprus Museum** (▷ 68), then follow the old city walls to Plateia Eleftherias at the top of Ledra Street (Odos Lidras, ▷ 69), a pedestrian-only shopping street where you can have coffee alfresco.

Mid-morning Visit **Leventis Municipal Museum** (▷ 74), before taking a stroll through **Laiki Geitonia** (▷ 74), a charming restored area home to tavernas and souvenir shops. Visit the **Ethnographical Museum** (▷ 73) at the splendid house of Hadjigeorgakis Kornesios, or admire the icons at the **Byzantine Museum** (▷ 73), or handicrafts and costumes at the adjoining Cyprus Folk Art Museum at the Makarios III Cultural Foundation.

Lunch Make your way to Laiki Geitonia for a pizza at **Il Forno** (▷ 83) or enjoy typical Cypriot dishes while people watching at **Kathodon** (▷ 83).

Afternoon Refuelled, stroll down Ledra Street and cross the now-opened border (Green Line; take your passports) to explore northern Nicosia. Head toward the minarets of **Selimiye Mosque** (▷ 97) to admire the magnificent architecture of this former 13th-century cathedral, then stroll across the square to the **Lapidary Museum** (▷ 101) before exploring the fascinating surrounding streets. The courtyard of the beautiful **Büyük Han** (▷ 100) is a good place to pick up souvenirs and have a drink.

Dinner A meal at lively, local favourite **Zanettos** (▷ 84), is a must. For something more romantic, try **Plaka** (▷ 84) on an attractive square in a southern Nicosia suburb.

Evening After dinner, join the locals for coffee or a nightcap at one of the many cafés and bars on Leoforos Archiepiskopou Makariou III, such as **Da Capo** (▷ 81) or **Mondo** (▷ 81).

DAY 2: PAFOS

Morning Kickstart the day by joining the locals for coffee on the terrace of a café before heading to the impressive **Tombs of the Kings** (▷ 53), which you'll want to explore early before it starts to get too hot.

Mid-morning Visit the engaging **District Archaeological Museum** (▷ 58), which will go a long way toward putting much of what you'll see in Pafos in context, before taking a look at the small but fascinating **Ethnographic Museum** (▷ 59).

Lunch There's no lovelier place to eat in Pafos than Theo's Seafood Restaurant on the waterfront, sitting in the sun and overlooking the attractive harbour. If you're more interested in the food than the views, then head to gourmet deli, **Gina's Place** (▷ 64), a favourite with the expat community.

Afternoon Visit the Pafos Fort (▷ 53) overlooking the harbour; the views are attractive from this vantage point, plus it's cool inside. Make your way to **Pafos Archaeological Park** (▷ 54) to enjoy the impressive Roman mosaics, Saranta Kolones and the ancient Odeon. You'll want to save the site until the sun has lost its sting, so if it's still too hot, have a stroll around the nearby pedestrianized area of Kato Pafos to browse the shops.

Dinner Pafos has excellent restaurants, but local favourites include **Mandra Tavern** (▷ 64) for lamb *kleftiko*, **Artio Brasserie** (▷ 64) for Mediterranean or the **O'Shin Sushi Bar** (▷ 64) for Japanese.

Evening Head back to the old harbour, a great place for a stroll on a balmy summer's evening when it's cooler than anywhere else in Pafos.

Top 25

TOP
25

► ► ►

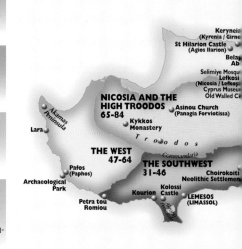

Keryneia
(Kyrenia / Girne)
St Hilarion Castle
(Agios Ilarion)
Belapais
Abbey
Selimiye Mosque
Lefkosia
(Nicosia / Lefkoşa)
Cyprus Museum
Old Walled City

NICOSIA AND THE HIGH TROODOS
65–84
Asinou Church
(Panagia Forviotissa)

Kykkos
Monastery

Akamas
Peninsula

Lara

T r o o d o s

THE WEST
47–64

Pafos
(Paphos)

Archaeological
Park

Petra tou
Romiou

Commandaria

THE SOUTHWEST
31–46

Kourion

Kolossi
Castle

Choirokoitia
Neolithic Settlement

LEMESOS
(LIMASSOL)

These pages are a quick guide to the Top 25, which are described in more detail later. Here they are listed alphabetically, and the tinted background shows which area they are in.

Famagusta ▷ **90–91**
Within its imposing Venetian walls is a city packed with historic sites.

Famagusta: Lala Mustafa Paşa Mosque ▷ **92**
A structure that marries a Latin church with a minaret.

Hala Sultan Tekke and Larnaka Salt Lake ▷ **24**
An important mosque in a perfect salt lake setting.

Kantara Castle ▷ **93**
A tumbledown castle set in splendid isolation with spectacular views.

Karpaz Peninsula ▷ **96**
Windswept beaches, Byzantine churches and small stone villages.

Kolossi Castle ▷ **36** A 13th-century tower surrounded by vineyards.

Kourion ▷ **37** A sprawling archaeological site in a magnificent setting with an impressive theatre.

Kyrenia: Harbour and Castle ▷ **94–95** Simply the most splendid harbour on the island.

Lara ▷ **52** Ripe for exploring, with remote untouched beaches and its famous sea turtles.

Larnaka ▷ **25** A palm tree-lined promenade, popular seafront cafés, and a long public beach.

Nicosia: Old Walled City ▷ **69** The 16th-century walls are impressive for their longevity and scale.

Nicosia: Cyprus Museum ▷ **68** Home to a wealth of objects from important sites across the island.

Limassol ▷ **38** Lively and sophisticated, with good beaches, great resorts and excellent restaurants.

Map labels:
Karpaz Peninsula
Kantara Castle
THE NORTH
85–106
entadaktylos (Besparmak)
Ammochostos (Famagusta) Bay
Salamis
Mesaoria (Mesarya)
Ammochostos (Famagusta / Gazimağusa)
Lala Mustafa Paşa Mosque
THE SOUTHEAST
20–30
arnaka alt Lake
Larnaka (Larnaca)
a Sultan Tekke

◀ ◀ ◀

Shopping

Cyprus may not be Milan, but then nor is shopping high on anyone's list of things to do on an island where sun, sand and sea take priority. While the island's shops provide an escape from the sun when temperatures soar, and are open late enough for you to have a quiet browse in the evening, some of the best things to buy are out of the cities in the villages.

Traditional Handicrafts

Cypriots still produce traditional handicrafts using techniques handed down through generations. A good source for textiles, pottery, olive-wood products, jewellery, baskets and other handicrafts is the government-run Cyprus Handicraft Centre. Ceramics, terracotta and earthenware pottery are best bought from the villages of Geroskipou, Koloni, Omodos and Foini in the south, and Kyrenia and Ortaköy in the north. At Omodos you'll find a range of handicrafts, including ceramics, glassware and textiles, making the town a great one-stop-shop if you don't have long on the island. Vibrant, striped, woven textiles are a good buy and make great wall hangings, tablecloths and bedcovers—Fyti is a good place to look. Colourful hand-woven reed baskets can be found in Liopetri, northern Nicosia, Sotira and Xylofagou.

Lace

Cyprus has a long tradition of creating exquisite handmade lace and embroidery, the most

LEFKARA LACE

Lefkara lace, known as *lefkaritika,* comes only from the village of Lefkara and is renowned around the world. The authentic lace is made using Irish linen (from Northern Ireland) and French cotton thread, and comes only in white, brown and ecru, in about ten designs, which is passed down through generations of the village's families from mother to daughter. The lace is reversible, meaning it looks perfect on both sides. There are three qualities: top-quality, standard and amateur, priced accordingly.

Cyprus abounds with traditional crafts that will make great souvenirs to take home

famous being *lefkaritika* from Lefkara, although lace is also made in other villages. If you're after *lefkaritika* then buy it at the source. Elsewhere you can't be certain you're getting the genuine article; watch out for the telltale 'Made in China' tags, or signs a tag has been removed.

Cypriot Wine

Cypriot wines have improved significantly in recent years. Cyprus boasts around 40 wineries and while the cellar door experience may not be as sophisticated as in France or Italy, most vineyards offer wine tastings and sell wine by bottles and cases. Look for signs for wineries as you drive around and make an effort to drop in. Wineries open daily to the public include Tsikkias, Kolios, Kamanterena, Vardalis, Vouni, and Zenon. Monasteries such as Kykkos and Chrysorrogiatissa also produce wines and are a great place to pick up some beautifully boxed bottles, including the local specialty Commandaria. You can also buy wine at the Cyprus Wine Museum (▷ 40).

Edible Souvenirs

Most Cypriot cities boast a good delicatessen or gourmet food store where you can buy delicious local specialties, such as herbed olives, olive oils, pickles and preserves, to take home. You'll also see stalls by the side of the road selling homemade fruit jams and honey fragrant from local herbs and flowers. Geroskipou specializes in *loukoumi*, the Cypriot version of Turkish Delight, which you'll see all over Cyprus.

A LOST ART RETURNS

While the Byzantine technique of religious icon painting nearly disappeared under Ottoman rule, there has been a recent resurgence in this intricate art. Today, icon painters are creating superb reproductions of classic icons using traditional techniques. Some monasteries have them for sale, such as Agia Varnava Monastery and Chrysorrogiatissa Monastery (▷ 56) among others.

Out and About

Many visitors come to Cyprus to laze about on the beach or by a swimming pool. Yet equally as enjoyable is exploring the island's splendid landscapes, whether it's the Troodos Mountains, forests and wild Arkamas Peninsula in the south, or the jagged dramatic Besparmak Mountains and breathtaking Karpaz Peninsula in the north.

Walks

Cyprus boasts superb walking opportunities. In the south, a comprehensive network of nearly 50 sign-posted walking tracks covers some 200km (121 miles). Described in nature trail brochures available from the Cyprus Tourism Organization (CTO), the routes pass through splendid scenery with spectacular views, picnic tables and gradients to suit all ages and levels of fitness, and most are circular. Popular walks include the 3km (1.75-mile) Kalidonia Trail near Platres, taking you to pretty waterfalls; the 3km (1.8-mile) Persephone Trail, beginning at Troodos town square and the 7km (4-mile) Artemis Trail at Mount Olympos.

Drives

Sealed roads criss-cross Cyprus making it a joy to explore. Most are in excellent condition, although they are often narrow and winding, so exercise caution. Routes with scenic vistas include the drive along the Karpaz Peninsula from Yenierenköy via Dipkarpaz to Zafer Burnu; the route from Pomos Point to Kato Pyrgos; and the Cedar Valley drive in the western Troodos.

RAMBLING, CYPRUS STYLE

Cyprus is a wonderful destination to do some rambling, or hiking, and the European long distance path (E4) now includes Cyprus. The path runs right across the centre of the country connecting Pafos and Larnaka airports as well as taking in the scenic Troodos Mountains and the Akamas Peninsula. You can thank the Greek Ramblers Association for Cyprus' inclusion, and you can pick up a brochure with basic maps from tourism offices on the island.

Exploring the island's countryside, whether energetically or in a more sedate way, is most rewarding

Cyprus by Night

Cypriots go out late and stay out late, so if you want to join the local action you'll have to make a habit of having an afternoon siesta. Evenings normally begin with a see-and-be-seen stroll, especially in seaside towns like Larnaka, Pafos and Kyrenia, followed by drinks on the terrace of a café or bar, dinner around 10pm, then a nightcap.

Sunset Strolling

Dress up and head to the square or seaside promenade to join the Cypriots on their sunset stroll. Locals love their evening saunter, especially in summer. The waterfront is where it's at in Larnaka, Limassol, Pafos and Kyrenia, while in Nicosia locals do laps of Ledra Street.

Café Culture

Cypriots love their cafés and settle in for hours chatting over coffee late into the night. Snag an alfresco terrace seat for the best people-watching. Larnaka has dozens of cafés opposite the beach, at their liveliest in the evening. At Pafos, Latchi (Lakki) and Kyrenia you can watch the boats bobbing in the water from harbourside cafés.

Bars and Pubs

Locals prefer chic bars over Irish pubs, which exist to please expats and visitors. Not big drinkers, they sit for a while, content to socialize. Lounge bars are popular, especially in Limassol and Larnaka. Nicosia's hip bars are mostly on Leoforos Archiepiskopou Makariou III.

Lively resorts or beautiful sunsets, Cyprus can deliver on all fronts when the sun goes down

---

CAFÉ LIFE

All Cypriots love their café life. Locals like to sit at their *kafeneion* and chat, taking turns sipping coffee and sipping the glass of water that's always served with local coffee. Greek or Turkish coffee consists of coffee beans ground to a fine powder and boiled up in a small pot with varying amounts of sugar added, as ordered by the customer. Note that the fine coffee grounds sit at the bottom of the cup, so don't drink it to the last drop.

Eating Out

Eating out in Cyprus ranges from a casual, paper napkin beachside shack to a sophisticated, white tablecloth city restaurant. Generic 'Greek' describes the common cuisine of the south while 'Turkish' is the standard in the north, however, then there's Cypriot cuisine, influenced by both.

When to Eat

Everything on Cyprus runs to a relaxed sense of time—dining is no exception. Breakfasts in hotels are generally from 7am to 11am and as breakfast is being cleared away, lunch is being set up. Tavernas and restaurants open for lunch from noon until 3 or 4pm and given the style of food, it can be a long affair. Dinner sees visitors weary from the sun eating from around 7pm, however, locals will book a table for 9 or 10pm.

Where to Eat

The question 'where to eat?' is usually answered with 'a table outside'. Alfresco dining by the seaside is wonderful in Cyprus, especially accompanied by fresh seafood and a crisp white wine. The most popular place to eat is a taverna, a casual eatery with indoor and outdoor seating featuring local dishes, supplemented with Cypriot specialties, and often a few international favourites such as burgers and pasta. Restaurants are more upmarket, often offering French or Italian food. Cafés will serve sandwiches, salads and the like, and there are also plenty of pubs and pizzerias.

WHAT TO EAT

A typical Cypriot meal starts with meze, which are little plates or dips, such as *taramasalata* (a paste of salted and cured cod's roe). Salads are often variations of the ubiquitous Greek salad, with tomatoes, cucumber, red onion and oregano topped with feta. Fish is generally grilled simply and meat dishes are often winter casseroles. In the north look out for 'full kebabs', a procession of meat dishes.

Experience tasty lunches at a seafront café or on the verandah of a mountain restaurant

Restaurants by Cuisine

There are restaurants, cafés, tavernas and bars to suit all tastes and budgets in Cyprus. For a more detailed description of each of our recommendations, see Cyprus by Area.

CAFÉS/BARS

Ammos (▷ 30)
Azafran (▷ 105)
Café Dükkan (▷ 105)
Gina's Place (▷ 64)
Maze (▷ 84)

ETHNIC

Akakiko (▷ 83)
Flavours of India (▷ 46)
Habibi (▷ 30)
Laughing Buddha (▷ 106)
Moti Mahal (▷ 30)
O'Shin Sushi Bar (▷ 64)
Pagoda (▷ 30)
Umi (▷ 30)

FINE DINING

Dionysos (▷ 46)
Mavrommatis (▷ 46)
Vivaldi (▷ 46)

GREEK CYPRIOT

Apollo Taverna (▷ 46)
Kathodon (▷ 83)
Mandra Tavern (▷ 64)
Mattheos (▷ 84)
Militzis (▷ 30)
Plaka (▷ 84)
Seven St. Georges (▷ 64)
To Paradosiako (▷ 30)
Zanettos (▷ 84)

INTERNATIONAL

Artio Brasserie (▷ 64)
Beige (▷ 46)
Chop't (▷ 83)
Erodos (▷ 83)
Mill Hotel Restaurant (▷ 84)
El Sabor Latino (▷ 106)
Sitio (▷ 84)
Yiolandel (▷ 84)

ITALIAN

Artima (▷ 46)
Caprice (▷ 46)
Cavaillini (▷ 64)
Cos'Altro (▷ 83)
Il Forno (▷ 83)

SEAFOOD

Lagoon Seafood Restaurant (▷ 106)
Latsi Fish Tavern (▷ 83)
Missina (▷ 106)
Saint George (▷ 64)
Varoshiotis Seafood (▷ 30)
Vassos (▷ 30)
Yiangos & Peter (▷ 64)

TURKISH CYPRIOT

The Address (▷ 105)
Bellapais Gardens Restaurant (▷ 105)
Cenap (▷ 105)
Cyprus House (▷ 105)
DB (▷ 105)
Harbour Club (▷ 106)
Lemon Tree (▷ 106)
Mirage (▷ 106)
Niazi's (▷ 106)
Pasha (▷ 106)

If You Like...

However you'd like to spend your time in Cyprus, these ideas should help you tailor your perfect visit. Each suggestion has a fuller write-up elsewhere in the book.

BEACH BASKING

Karpaz Peninsula (▷ 96) boasts the island's most breathtakingly beautiful beach, backed by windswept sand dunes, near Galounopetra Point.
Avdimou (▷ 40) is a lovely sand and pebble beach backed by chalky cliffs and split by a small picturesque headland.
Lara Beach (▷ 52) on the remote west coast is a long stretch of beautiful creamy sands.

Karpas Peninsula (above); St. Hilarion Castle (below)

SPECTACULAR VISTAS

Petrou tou Romiou (▷ 39), viewed from the lookout to the east, is Cyprus' most photographed vista for a reason.
St. Hilarion Castle (▷ 98) offers heavenly views with your head literally in the clouds.
Pomos Point (▷ 59) promises it will just be you and the mountain goats marvelling at the magnificent scenery from this remote vantage point.

A BREATH OF FRESH AIR

On Mount Olympos (▷ 70) the air doesn't get fresher than this, especially in winter.
At Kantara Castle (▷ 93) breathe in the mountain air before the wind sweeps you off your feet.
At Cedar Valley (▷ 70), inhale the fragrance of pine as you cruise through the ancient forest.

Artemis trail (above); local wines (below)

TASTING WINE

Learn about the world's oldest wine at Cyprus Wine Museum (▷ 40).
Buy superb Cypriot wines from the cellar door at an ever-increasing number of wineries (▷ 11) open to the public.
Sip Commandaria made by the monks at Kykkos Monastery (▷ 72).

ourion (below)

AMBLING ANCIENT SITES

Enjoy the drama of the spectacular coastal vistas and daring hang-gliders from the ancient theatre at Kourion (▷ 37).

Explore underground burial chambers and passages cut deep in the ground at the Tombs of the Kings (▷ 53).

Wander along atmospheric colonnades of marble columns at ancient Salamis (▷ 99).

*agers chatting
a café in Polis (above)*

A TASTE OF TRADITION

Have coffee at a local *kafeneion* (▷ panel 13) or coffee shop where you can join the old guys in a game of backgammon or cards.

Visit the Bandabulya (▷ 103) to buy your Turkish Delight, dates and preserves to take home.

Enjoy *ouzo* or *raki* with your meze (▷ 14) instead of a beer or wine.

SPECIALTY SHOPPING

Watch skilful lacemakers lovingly embroider *lefkaritika* lace in the charming village of Lefkara (▷ 10, 41).

Buy floral and acacia-scented honey from stalls by the side of the road (▷ 11).

Take home boxes of sweet *loukoumi* or Turkish Delight from Geroskipou (▷ 11, panel 103) in the south or from the market in the old town of northern Nicosia.

*ce-making (above); Troodos
untains (below)*

SAVING FOR A RAINY DAY

Pack a picnic and enjoy lunch in the Troodos Mountains (▷ 70).

Linger over a coffee at a stylish café for a while, as the locals do, and enjoy some people-watching for free (▷ 13).

Enjoy happy hour drinks at the bars near the beach in Agia Napa (▷ 26).

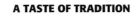

SPA PAMPERING

Nourish your skin with a traditional Cypriot treatment of olive oil and honey at the hotel Anassa's luxurious spa (▷ 112).
Energize with shiatsu and *oshibori* (warm Japanese towels) at the chic Shiseido Spa at the Four Seasons Hotel (▷ panel 112).
Re-hydrate with an After-Sun Ceremony at Columbia Beach Resort's opulent bathhouse style spa (▷ 112).

Indulge yourself at a spa or luxury hotel (above and be...)

GORGEOUS HOTEL GETAWAYS

Relax on your private rooftop terrace in a Kyma Suite while someone takes care of the kids at the chic Almyra hotel (▷ 112).
Stroll the fragrant Mediterranean gardens or sit back and relax on your balcony overlooking the sea at the lavish Anassa hotel (▷ 112).
Hang out in the hip lobby bar with the chic locals at the island's coolest hotel, the Londa (▷ 112).

GASTRONOMIC DELIGHTS

Marvel at the creative flavour combinations of the contemporary Cypriot cuisine at Mavromatis (▷ 46).
Delight in the exquisite presentation of the adventurous cuisine at Dionysos (▷ 46).
Enjoy Mediterranean cuisine with a twist at stylish Caprice (▷ 46).

Creative chefs at work (above); streetside café i... Limassol (below)

CAFÉ-CRUISING AND BAR-HOPPING

Soak up the sun at one of Limassol's little alfresco seaside cafés (▷ 38) and kiosks.
Enjoy a sunset drink by the water at the old harbour of Kyrenia (▷ 94).
Bar hop between Nicosia's stylish bars centred on and around Leoforos Archiepiskopou Makariou III (▷ 13).

Cyprus by Area

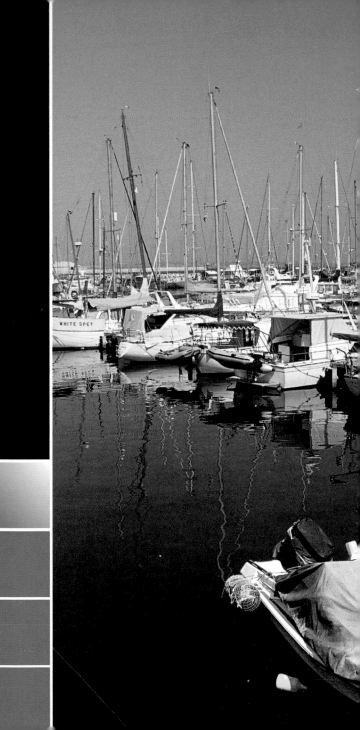

The Southeast

Once Cyprus' scenic rural heartland, agriculture in the southeast has long ago been supplanted by tourism. While Agia Napa and Protaras have been somewhat spoilt by development, the low-key city of Larnaka (Larnaca) is appealing and its seaside promenade is a wonderful place to be.

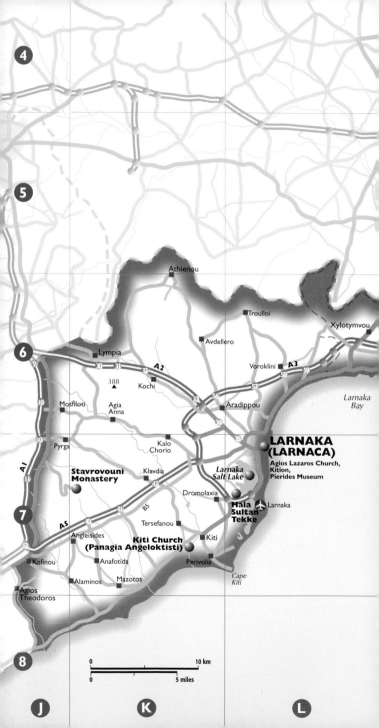

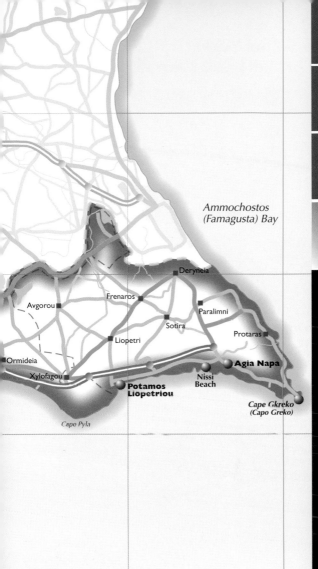

Ammochostos
(Famagusta) Bay

Deryneia

Frenaros

Avgorou

Paralimni

Sotira

Protaras

Liopetri

Agia Napa

Ormideia

Nissi
Beach

Xylofagou

**Potamos
Liopetriou**

*Cape Gkreko
(Capo Greko)*

Capo Pyla

Hala Sultan Tekke and Larnaka Salt Lake

The domed mosque, inside and out (left, middle); a view across the salt lake (right)

THE BASICS

➕ L7

✉ Odos Kiti, 3km (2 miles) west of Larnaka, near airport

🕐 Jun–Aug daily 8–7.30; Apr–May, Sep–Oct 8–6; Nov–Mar 8–5

🚌 Bus from Larnaka stops on the main road

♿ Few

✋ Free

HIGHLIGHTS

● View of the mosque from across the salt lake
● The mosque's pine and palm-filled garden
● Elegant minaret and silver dome
● Pink flamingoes, if you're lucky to see them on the lake

TIP

● Visit early morning or late afternoon to take advantage of the golden light reflecting on the salt lake.

On the edge of a shimmering salt lake, in pine and palm-filled gardens, the setting for this important Muslim holy shrine must be one of the most enchanting of any sight on the island.

Wonderful sight There's no denying the view of this elegant sandstone mosque from across the salt lake is stunning. It's especially so early in the morning or at dusk when the sunlight creates a shimmering effect on the pink-hued salt lake, contrasting nicely with the mosque's silvery-blue dome and delicate silver-topped minaret.

Place of worship While non-Muslim visitors may stop to enjoy the vista for sheer aesthetic reasons, and perhaps pay a visit to the mosque to escape the heat with a stroll through its peaceful, leafy gardens, the Hala Sultan Tekke is very important to true Muslims and is a place of great religious significance.

Holy shrine The mosque's importance is undisputed because it's here that the prophet Mohammed's maternal aunt, Umm Haram was buried in AD649 after falling from a donkey and breaking her neck while participating in an Arab raid on Cyprus. Marked by three simple stones, her modest grave is a place of pilgrimage. The mosque was built in 1816 by the Ottoman Turks, while the tomb of Umm Haram dates from 1760. Non-Muslims can enter the understated mosque, but like Muslims, should remove their shoes and dress modestly; women should wear a headscarf.

Larnaka seafront (left); the fort's stone walls (middle) conceal a medieval museum (right)

Larnaka

Lovely Larnaka (Larnaca), with its pretty tree-lined promenade, alfresco cafés and seafront tavernas, is one of the island's most attractive towns. Its old town and fascinating museums add to the appeal.

Character The southeast's commercial capital, Larnaka sees fewer tourists checking into its hotels than nearby Agia Napa and fewer expats moving in compared to Protaras. Yet the lively town has a lot more character than its eastern neighbours. Locals like to linger in the cafés along pretty palm tree-lined Finikoudes Promenade or enjoy long seafood lunches at the tavernas on Mackenzie Beach. The sandy town beach is a perfect place to spend the day, if not sunbathing or swimming, then joining a game of beach volleyball. Once the sun loses its sting, the thing to do is simply stroll.

Old town With its atmospheric sandstone architecture and ramshackle charm, Larnaka's delightful yet diminutive Skala or old town is worth wandering, especially in the late afternoon. Artists and craftspeople work out of tiny workshops and there are small galleries, design stores and gift shops.

Main sights Aside from Agios Lazaros Church, absorbing Pierides Museum and the Kition (▷ 27) ruins, Larnaka's other key sight is its Turkish fort. Built in 1625, the imposing stone castle was a prison and army barracks during British rule. Its medieval museum has a small collection of relics, yet it's the fort's location on the shore with the waves lapping its walls that makes it appealing.

THE BASICS

⊞ L7
🛈 Plareia Vasileos Pavlou, tel 2465 4322
Lanarka Fort and Museum
☎ 2432 2710
🕐 Nov–Mar daily 8–5; Apr–May, Sep–Oct 8–6; Jun–Aug 8–7.30
🍴 Restaurants and cafés nearby
♿ Few
💲 Inexpensive
Municipality Walking Tours
☎ 2476 5755
💲 Free

HIGHLIGHTS

● Larnaka's tiny Skala
● Agios Lazaros Church and its elegant arcade (▷ 26)
● Fascinating Pierides Museum (▷ 27)
● Turkish Fort and Medieval Museum
● Cafés on palm tree-lined Finikoudes Promenade
● Mackenzie Beach seafood tavernas

More to See

AGIA NAPA

The island's most popular beach resort once had ambitions to be the Eastern Mediterranean's dance club capital. The beautiful young clubbers have moved on, but it's still popular with UK and Scandinavian families and retirees, and in summer a hardcore drinking crowd. The 16th-century monastery on the town square and the state-of-the-art Thalassa Museum of the Sea are impressive.

✚ N6 ✉ 43km (27 miles) east of Larnaka 🍴 Restaurants and cafés

CAPO GREKO

The scenery at Cape Greko (Karo Gkreko) is dramatic and views down to the rocky bays and crystal clear water are beautiful on a sunny day.

✚ P6 ✉ 8km (5 miles) southeast of Agia Napa 🚶 None 🖐 Free

KITI CHURCH

Constructed in the 11th century on the ruins of a 5th-century church, its Greek name, Panagia Angeloktisti, means 'built by angels' and the beautiful mosaic, depicting angels watching over the Virgin Mary as she nurses Christ, is the main attraction.

✚ K7 ✉ Mazatos, edge of Kiti village ☎ 2442 4646 🕐 Daily 7.30–12, 2–4; if locked ask for key at the café 🍴 Café nearby 🚶 Few 🖐 Free; donation welcome

LARNAKA: AGIOS LAZAROS CHURCH

www.ayioslazaros.org

It is said that Saint Lazarus, Larnaka's patron saint, was resurrected by Christ, lived here for 30 years and was ordained Bishop of Kition by saints Barnabas and Mark. The church was built in the 9th century over his stone tomb. which can still be seen inside, it was restored in the 17th century. The exterior with its elegant arcades is gorgeous, although the extravagantly decorated interior should not be missed, too. There is also a small Byzantine Museum with some icons.

✚ L7 ✉ Odos Agiou Lazarou ☎ 2465 2498 🕐 Daily 7.30–5.30 🍴 Cafés nearby 🚶 Few 🖐 Church free; museum inexpensive

St. Lazarus Church, Larnaka

Iconostasis inside Kiti Church

LARNAKA: KITION

Ancient Kition's ruins are scattered across Larnaka but the Leontiou Machaira site, near the Archaeological Museum, has the most intact structures—with imagination you can make out the base of a Phoenician Temple.
🔲 L7 ✉ Odos Leontiou Machaira ☎ 2430 4115 ⏰ Mon–Wed and Fri 8–2.30, Thu 8–5; closed Sat–Sun 🍴 Restaurants and cafés nearby ♿ Few 💵 Inexpensive

LARNAKA: PIERIDES MUSEUM

www.pieridesfoundation.com.cy
The staggering display of archaeological finds, Byzantine and medieval relics, ancient Greek and Roman glassware and sculpture was the Pierides family's private collection, housed in their elegant former home.
🔲 L7 ✉ 4 Odos Zinonos Kitieos ☎ 2481 4555 ⏰ Mon–Thu 9-4, Fri–Sat 9–1
🍴 Restaurants and cafés nearby ♿ Good 💵 Inexpensive

NISSI BEACH

While some blame Nissi for the southeast's relentless tacky development, to others it's their beloved Nissi that they return to year after year. Expect an array of watersports and sun beds and crystal-clear water.
🔲 N6 ✉ 2km (1.2 miles) west of Agia Napa 🍴 Restaurants and cafés nearby

POTAMOS LIOPETRIOU

A tranquil spot, little more than a creek with wooden jetties where fishing boats dock, two seafood tavernas, a small sandy beach and a longer, narrow stretch of rock and sand.
🔲 M6 ✉ 14km (8.5 miles) west of Agia Napa 🍴 Tavernas by beach

STAVROVOUNI MONASTERY

Stavrovouni means 'mother of the Cross'. The 'mother' was that of Constantine the Great, Empress Saint Helena, who brought a fragment from the Cross of Jesus here from Jerusalem in AD327. Stunningly sited at 690m (2,263ft), there are spectacular views. Women aren't allowed to enter.
🔲 K7 ✉ 40km (25 miles) west of Larnaka ⏰ Daily 8–12, 3–6 ♿ None 💵 Free

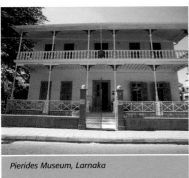

Pierides Museum, Larnaka

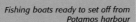

Fishing boats ready to set off from Potamos harbour

Shopping

ASCOTT POTTERY

A pottery shop, selling beautifully produced ceramics. You'll find both traditional Cypriot designs as well as modern interpretations and the kids can have a go at the pottery wheel while you take your time browsing.

⊞ N6 ✉ 210 Leoforos Protaras, Paralimni ☎ 2382 2428

ATHOS ICONS

Head here for your more monastic souvenirs, from Byzantine music, stunning hand-painted icons, and heady incense and fine wines from Athos Monastery.

⊞ L7 ✉ 39 Grigoris Afxentiou, Larnaka ☎ 2462 6256

DODICI

www.dodici.gr
Girls love these Greek-made shoes, which are a bit different to those you'll find back home. Expect all styles, from trendy casuals to the ultra glam.

⊞ L7 ✉ 173 Odos Ermou, Larnaka ☎ 2482 3950

EMIRA POTTERY

While you'll find pottery and ceramics in traditional styles here, Emira is a favourite among pottery fans for their more unusual designs. If you can't see anything you like, you can always order something.

⊞ L7 ✉ 13 Mehmet Ali, Larnaka ☎ 2462 3952

JOAKIM JEWELLERY

Joakim can make a full range of jewellery to your design, whether precious metals or gem encrusted. The shop stocks unique pieces designed in house and also imports designer ranges such as Gucci and Roberto Cavalli.

⊞ L7 ✉ 22a Zenonos Kitieou ☎ 2465 4394

MARKS & SPENCER

Forgot to pack your bikinis? Need some hiking socks? A beach towel perhaps? This popular (and great value) British department store is a good place to start looking for high-quality basics. Locals love it just as much as homesick expats. Larnaka has another branch at Zinonos Kitieous.

⊞ L7 ✉ Stratigou Timaya, Larnaka ☎ 2466 1517

CHIC LARNAKA

Larnaka's main shopping area is rather chic with stylish youthful fashion boutiques such as Zara and Mango alongside more exclusive designer stores like Armani and Fendi. Timinis boutique stocks Versace and Boss, while 34 The Shop is the place to head for Paul Frank, Paul Smith, Replay and Allstra. You'll also find a Debenhams and Marks & Spencer (▷ above) here. Most shops are on Odos Ermou and Stratigou Timaya.

MAVROS

The eager staff here are happy to help search out what you need in this cluttered store stocking everything from camping and fishing gear to sporting goods and diving equipment.

⊞ L7 ✉ 35 Odos Ermou, on the corner of Galileo, Larnaka ☎ 2482 8872

OAK TREE WINE CELLAR

www.katoditiswines.com
Owned by Katodritis Wines, this is one of Cyprus' best wine shops (their motto after all is 'because life is too short to drink only ordinary wines'). The extensive range of Cypriot wines makes it the place to head for your liquid souvenirs or a bottle of white to have with your takeaway fish and chips.

⊞ L7 ✉ 99G Odos Drousioti, Larnaka ☎ 2481 5044

THEOPHANIDES EYEWORLD

Cypriots love their chic sunnies and glasses—the more attention-grabbing they are the better—and this is the place to head for the latest eyewear and bargains at the end of season sales.

⊞ N6 ✉ 18 Leoforus Archiepiskopou Makariou III, Agia Napa ☎ 2372 1490

Entertainment and Activities

INTERYACHTING CATAMARAN CRUISES

www.interyachting.com.cy
Enjoy a leisurely cruise on a twin-hulled catamaran (more stable) to Famagusta Bay, stopping on the way to swim or snorkel in the crystal clear water. Buffet lunches are included. The sunset cruise is pretty special.

N6 ✉ Protaras Harbour ☎ 2581 1900

KARTING CENTER

www.kartingcenter.com.cy
This state-of-the-art mini go-kart track is specifically designed with kids in mind, with automatic settings and adjustable speeds depending on your child's age, plus some twin-seat go-karts so parents can join their little ones.

L7 ✉ Dromolaxia, near Larnaka ☎ 7000 7677

LIQUID

www.liquidcafebar.com
This modish café-bar with its big comfy leather sofas is the favourite of the local style set. With its light airy feel, it's an ideal spot to sip a cocktail and for some Sunday afternoon people watching.

N6 ✉ 8 Kryou Nerou, Agia Napa ☎ 2381 9276

MAZOTOS CAMEL PARK

www.camel-park.com
While the kids love riding the long-lashed camels, a visit here is a good excuse for the adults to get out into the gorgeous countryside around the picturesque village of Mazotos. The Park also has a small museum, café and even a swimming pool.

K7 ✉ Larnaka–Mazotos road, Mazotos village ☎ 2499 1243

TIMES MUSIC BAR

What everyone loves about this place is can call in anytime of the day or night, for coffee in the morning, a cold beer in the afternoon, or cocktails in the evening. Things liven up at night when there might be jazz one evening and dance music another.

L/ ✉ Finikoudes Promenade, Larnaka ☎ 2462 5066

TOURIST SUBMARINE

This air-conditioned underwater submarine takes you to the bottom of the sea to see the Zenobia shipwreck, considered one of the world's best wrecks for diving. Hotel transfers can be organized.

IN SEASON ONLY

Be warned if you come off season—most leisure activities and entertainment are only offered in high season, from April to September. A lot of bars and dance clubs are closed during winter, especially in Agia Napa.

L7 ✉ Larnaka Marina ☎ 2465 6949

UNDERSEA ADVENTURES

www.underseawalkers.com
Stroll on the seabed—really—to get up close and personal with the marine life. There's no need for diving equipment or snorkels as air is pumped into a massive helmet. Enormously popular. Discounts for online bookings.

N6 ✉ De Costa Bay, Protaras ☎ 9956 3506

VIKING DIVERS

www.viking-divers.com
Arguably the best diving and water sports specialists on the island, this PADI 5-star centre offers certified diving courses, equipment rental, diving tours, boat safaris and snorkelling, along with a myriad of other water-based activities from parasailing to windsurfing.

L7 ✉ 2 Ithakis, Larnaka-Dekeleia road, Larnaka ☎ 2464 4676

YELLOW SUBMARINE

If you aren't keen on snorkelling or diving, but want to be able to enjoy the underwater scenery, hop in one of these air-conditioned surface submarines. There are reclining deck chairs and a bar, and you can swim if you want to.

N6 ✉ Agia Napa Harbour, in front of Vassos ☎ 9965 8280

Restaurants

PRICES

Prices are approximate, based on a 3-course meal for one person.

€€€	over €60
€€	€20–60
€	under €20

AMMOS (€)

www.ammos.eu

There are few better spots on a summer's day than Ammos, which, with its white wooden furniture, hammocks and sun beds, has a lovely relaxing atmosphere. It's almost as if the fresh, light, healthy cuisine is a welcome added extra.

⊞ L7 ✉ Mackenzie Beach, Larnaca ☎ 2482 8844 ⏰ Daily lunch, dinner

HABIBI (€)

This buzzy Lebanese restaurant serves tasty, terrific-value Arabic meze, and gets very busy on weekends when there's a belly-dancing show.

⊞ L7 ✉ 7 Efesou, Larnaca ☎ 7000 3222 ⏰ Daily lunch, dinner

MILITZIS (€€)

A longstanding favourite, this traditional taverna has plenty of atmosphere with its roughhewn walls and traditional checked tablecloths, but it's the delicious Cypriot specialties people keep coming back for.

⊞ L7 ✉ Piale Pasa, Larnaca ☎ 2465 5867 ⏰ Daily lunch, dinner

MOTI MAHAL (€)

Causing quite a stir when it first opened—the Rajhastani décor was a touch too exotic for Larnaca—this is now a stalwart on the promenade scene. It's not only good in the looks department, the Indian-fusion cuisine is tasty indeed.

⊞ L7 ✉ Finikoudes Promenade, Larnaca ☎ 7000 4484 ⏰ Daily lunch, dinner

PAGODA (€€)

Overlook the fact that this is part of a chain (albeit a stylish one at that) because the authentic Chinese cuisine at Pagoda is superb. Be sure to book in summer and on weekend nights.

⊞ N6 ✉ 29 Leoforos Nissi, Agia Napa ☎ 2381 9988 ⏰ Daily lunch, dinner

TO PARADOSIAKO (€)

This traditional seaside taverna is beloved by

SPECIALTIES

Look out for the following delicious local specialties on the menu:

Anthoi—sweet zucchini flowers stuffed with minced meat, rice, onions and herbs.

Loukanika—smoked pork sausages seasoned with wine and spices.

Tsamarella—dried goat meat liberally sprinkled with salt.

Zalatina—pork preserved in vinegar, orange juice and chilli.

locals and expats alike for its rustic and generously sized portions of delicious Cypriot and Greek food.

⊞ L7 ✉ 2 Sakaria, Mackenzie Beach, Larnaca ☎ 2465 8318 ⏰ Daily lunch, dinner

UMI (€€)

This chic and sleek fourth-floor Japanese eatery boasts brilliant sea views and the best sushi in Cyprus.

⊞ N6 ✉ Grecian Park Hotel, Protaras ☎ 2384 4044 ⏰ Daily dinner only

VAROSHIOTIS SEAFOOD (€€)

www.varoshiotis.com

Renowned across Cyprus for its beautifully-presen-ted fresh seafood, this chic family-owned Cypriot franchise lives up to its reputation, and is very popular. The waterfront location makes it an unbeatable lunch choice on a sunny day.

⊞ L7 ✉ Piale Pasa, Larnaca ☎ 7000 3536 ⏰ Daily lunch, dinner

VASSOS (€)

www.vassosfishrest.com

Overlooking the beach, the enormous interior is filled with big tables of local families feasting on platters of whole fish and bowls of salad, while the expats and tourists tuck into their fried seafood on the terrace outside.

⊞ N6 ✉ Harbour, Agia Napa ☎ 2372 1884 ⏰ Daily lunch, dinner

The Southwest

This is one of the most rewarding areas on Cyprus, with everything from the birthplace of a goddess along a magnificent coastline to medieval castles and significant archaeological sites, while bustling Limassol (Lemesos) boasts the island's best restaurants, buzzy bars and excellent shopping.

4

5

6

7

8

9

D

E

F

Koilani

Agios Mamas

Commandaria Ch

Vouni

Limnatis

732 ▲ Apsi

Agios Therapon

Korfi

Apesia

Pachna

Pano Kivides

Alassa

Fas

Chapotami

Anogyra

B8

Palc

Sotira

Ag Fyla

Alektora

Avdimou

Koutis

Kantou

Polemidia

A6

Ypsonas

Cyprus Wine Museum

Erimi

Kolossi Castle

Petra tou Romiou

Pissouri

Avdimou Beach

Kourion

Episkopi

L_ M B

Pissouri Bay

Avdimou Bay

Episkopi Bay

Akrotiri Peninsula

0   10 km

0   5 miles

Cape Zevgari

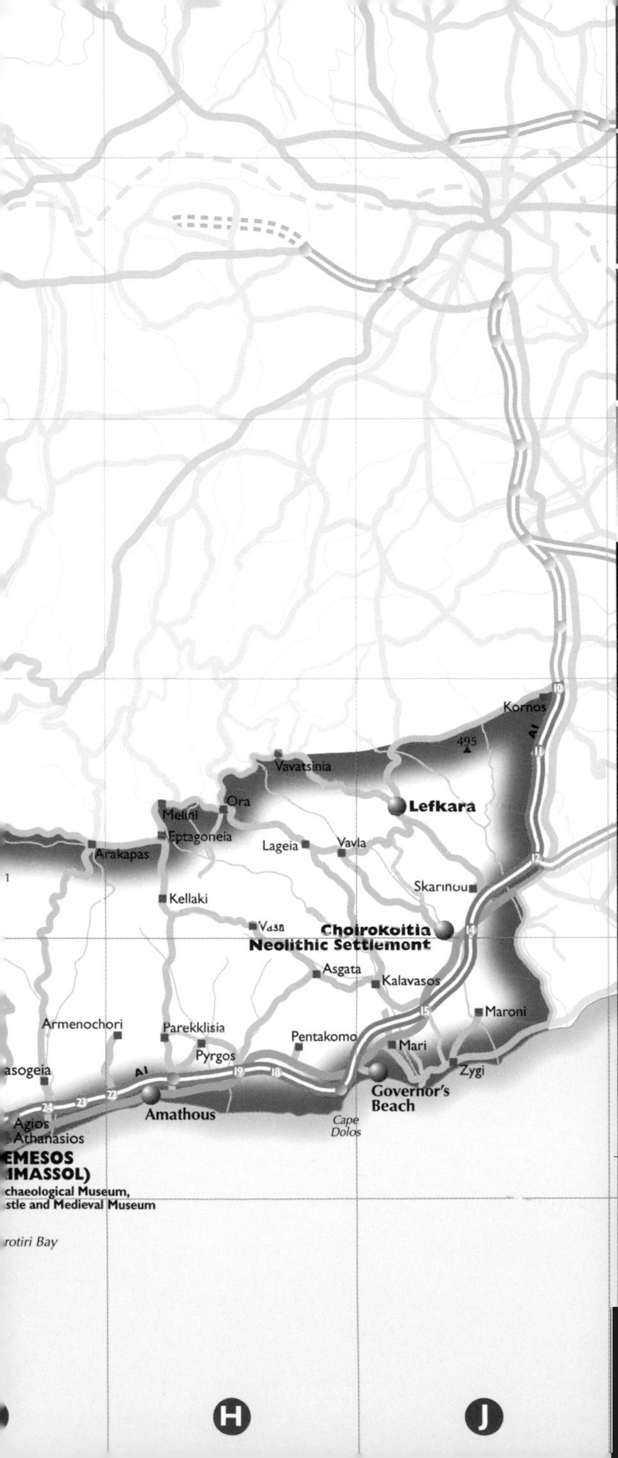

Kornos

495

Vavatsinia

Lefkara

Melini

Ora

Eptagoneia

Arakapas

Lageia   Vavla

Skarinou

Kellaki

Vasa

Choirokoitia
Neolithic Settlement

Asgata

Kalavasos

Armenochori

Parekklisia

Pentakomo

Maroni

asogeia

Pyrgos

Mari

Agios
Athanasios

Amathous

Governor's
Beach

Zygi

EMESOS
(IMASSOL)
chaeological Museum,
stle and Medieval Museum

Cape
Dolos

rotiri Bay

H   **J**

Choirokoitia Neolithic Settlement

Remains of original stone dwellings (left and opposite) and reconstructions (right)

THE BASICS

✚ J7
✉ Off junction 14 Nicosia–Limassol motorway, near Limassol
☎ 2432 2710
🕐 Jun–end Aug daily 8–7.30; Apr–end May, Sep–end Oct 8–6; Nov–end Mar 8–5
🍴 Restaurants and cafés within driving distance
♿ None
💷 Inexpensive

HIGHLIGHTS

● Impressive remains of two beehive-shaped houses
● Views looking down onto the site from the hill above

The oldest archaeological site on the island might not be its most striking or immediately impressive, but the ruins of the beehive houses that remain give a sense of life here from 6800BC.

Important site The site of Choirokoitia, which was once home to around 200 inhabitants who farmed the nearby land, was occupied from the 7th to the 4th century BC. The archaeological site is one of the most important prehistoric sites in the eastern Mediterranean and is a listed UNESCO World Heritage site. The finds from the ruins have given archaeologists much information about life during the occupation of the place—especially in relation to proto-urban settlements—and it's still rich with more to be discovered.

Beehive houses The beehive-shaped houses are the most recognizable feature of the site and are in two sizes, one spanning 4m (13ft) and the other 8m (26ft). The clearly crowded houses were linked and each 'house' served different purposes such as sleeping, cooking or storage. The inhabitants buried their dead underneath their houses and some houses show evidence of up to eight different periods of occupation.

View from above Archaeologists consider the site to be well preserved, however, visitors without an archaeological bent might beg to differ. The best view of the settlement is from the top of the hill where you can get a sense of the layout of one of the earliest examples of 'urban' living.

Kolossi Castle

The machicolations and crenels of Kolossi Castle

THE BASICS

✚ F8
✉ 14.5km (9 miles) from Limassol
☎ 2593 4907
🕐 Jun–end Aug daily 8–7.30; Apr–end May, Sep–end Oct 8–6; Nov–end Mar 8–5
🍴 Kiosk at site
🚌 Bus from Limasol
♿ None
🎫 Inexpensive

HIGHLIGHTS

● Imposing castle structure
● Enormous cavernous spaces within the castle
● Fascinating views across the orchards and vineyards from the roof
● The beautiful mural (now behind glass) located on the ground floor

Standing in an area full of fruit orchards and vineyards, striking Kolossi Castle was the headquarters of the Knights Hospitaller, a Crusader order, who built the first fortress in the late 13th century.

Sugary past Kolossi castle was of strategic importance to the Knights Hospitaller as well as providing a base from which to process sugar, an important export from that time. Also of importance was the production of Commandaria wine—fortified wine from local grape varieties grown around the castle's region. The castle suffered from a number of attacks by Egyptian Mamluk raiders in the 14th century and the buildings visible today date from the rebuilding, which took place in the 15th century. The Ottomans took it over in 1570 and sugar production continued until 1799.

Visiting the fortress Enter the castle over the tiny drawbridge into a pleasant Mediterranean garden and then proceed into the keep, which has walls 2.75m (9ft) thick and is three storeys high. From this robust structure, defenders were able to pour boiling oil from the parapet on to the attackers below. Much of the ground floor was used as a storage area. The first floor has two large rooms and a kitchen. On the second floor were the apartments of the Grand Commander, which have an airy feel created by four large windows. A spiral staircase leads to the roof, from which there are good views. The large vaulted building in the grounds was where the sugar cane was processed.

The amphitheatre (left); magnificent views from the site (middle); detail of a mosaic (right)

Kourion

In a wonderful setting, sprawling across a hilltop, Kourion is the most important archaeological site in the Greek Cypriot south. Impressively perched on the cliffs, the ancient city overlooks the sea.

Early beginnings Settlements have existed here since 3300BC although the first significant town was thought to have been established by the Mycenaeans around 1400BC. Kourion was at its peak under the Romans and it is that influence that is the most evident in the ruins. Thereafter, it went into decline, suffering from the attentions of Arab raiders, which saw its population move inland.

Discoveries Excavations have been ongoing here since 1873. The theatre has a striking setting with spectacular sea vistas. Once seating an audience of 3,500, it was probably built for displays of gladiatorial combat. Impressively restored, today it serves a less ferocious purpose of hosting summer performances of plays and concerts. Uphill from the theatre, the Annexe of Eustolios has an impressive mosaic floor, while further up are the baths, which follow the traditional Roman forum with a *frigidarium* (cold room) followed by a *tepidarium* (warm room) then a *caldarium* (hot baths). At the top of the hill is the Building of the Achilles Mosaic, what must have once been a very splendid house, dating from about AD4. A similar house lies nearby, where a mosaic shows two gladiators in combat. Also visible are the remains of an aqueduct that brought water to the Fountain House and a 5th-century Basilica.

THE BASICS

🔹 F8
✉ Off the Limassol–Pafos road
☎ 2593 4250
🕐 Apr–end May, Sep–end Oct 8–6; Jun–end Aug 8–7.30; Nov–end Mar 8–5
🍴 Kiosk on site
🚌 Bus from Limassol and Pafos
♿ Few
💰 Inexpensive
❓ Map of site at ticket office

HIGHLIGHTS

● Beautifully-preserved theatre with spectacular sea vistas
● Splendid mosaics in the Annexe of Eustolios, the baths and Building of the Achilles Mosaic
● Enjoying the spectacle of the hang-gliders swooping past the site

Limassol

Limassol's Old Town shops at night (left); Greek dancers in a Limassol club (right)

THE BASICS

✚ G8
ℹ 115A Odos Spirou Araouzou, tel 2536 2756

Limassol (Lemesos) is the island's most sophisticated and liveliest city, making up for its lack of beaches with a variety of superb seaside resorts, sublime gourmet restaurants, stylish cafés, bars and clubs, and excellent shopping opportunities.

HIGHLIGHTS

● Fascinating castle and medieval museum
● Atmospheric old town with an air of decay
● Lively and attractive seaside promenade
● Superb shopping opportunities
● Gastronomic restaurants
● Stylish cafés and bars

TIP

● Even if you're not bar-hopping or clubbing, Limassol's old centre is worth a stroll on a weekend evening for the lively atmosphere.

Humble beginnings The Knights Hospitaller developed Limassol as a trading post based on the export of Commandaria wine, which they made in the vineyards surrounding Kolossi. However, it wasn't until the 19th century when its major asset, the deep-water port, was fully utilized that the town grew into a significant commercial centre.

Tourist invasion Today, the road into town from Larnaka is lined with hotels and beach resorts, many of which are amongst the island's best. While a significant number of the businesses along this stretch are tourist-focused, pockets of sophistication cater for moneyed locals and more discerning visitors. The good shopping (especially around Odos Agiou Andreou), gastronomic restaurants and great nightlife also cater for these markets. The spring carnival and the wine festival in September are the liveliest times to visit.

Just explore Limassol's main historical site is its castle and medieval museum. There are also a few mosques with pretty minarets, serving as reminders of a time when Limassol had a Turkish quarter, but the best thing to do is simply wander. Explore the backstreets of the atmospheric old town, and walk the lively seaside boardwalk.

Petra tou Romiou

The Rock of Aphrodite, stunning under a sunset and enthralling in daylight

Striking chalky rocks set against a splendid turquoise sea, a sandy beach and a backdrop of white cliffs—there are few sites on the island that can claim to be as romantic and as evocative as the Rock of Aphrodite.

Perfect picture Petra tou Romiou, (the Rock of Romios), better known as the Rock of Aphrodite, is one of the most photographed sites on the island and with good reason—it's sublime. There are several places to stop for that postcard snap—one is close to the rock just back from the shore, near the car park; another is higher up on the cliff, where there's a tourist pavilion; and the best view is coming from Limassol, from the parking bay at the final bend before the road starts to descend.

Legend has it According to legend, this was the birthplace of the goddess of love, Aphrodite (or Venus to the Romans), who emerged—fully formed and exceptionally nubile—from the foaming sea. As beautifully evocative as this might be, the alleged events leading up to her birth (Cronus castrating Uranus and tossing his severed genitals into the sea) are less so.

Take a dip While the setting is lovely viewed from a distance, the beach itself is rather shingly, and not ideal for swimming due to riptides and rough water around the rocks. But it's worth stopping to soak up the magical atmosphere. And who can resist dipping their toes in the water where the goddess of love allegedly emerged?

THE BASICS

✚ D8

✉ 24km (15 miles) from Pafos

🚌 No restrictions

🍴 A café at the tourist pavilion and kiosk closer to the rock

♿ None

HIGHLIGHTS

● Viewing the Rock from all three vantage points
● Sunset vistas from the restaurant at the tourist pavilion
● Letting the waters that gave birth to the goddess of love lap over your bare feet

THE SOUTHWEST

★

TOP 25

More to See

AKROTIRI PENINSULA

It's not Cyprus' most attractive beach, with the container ships lined up waiting to dock at port off-shore, but locals love this long stretch of dark sand and pebbles, and the no-nonsense oceanfront tavernas. A short drive from the southern end of the beach, the 13th-century Agios Nikoloas ton Gaton (St. Nicholas of the Cats) monastery has fine mosaics and felines loafing about the place.

➕ F9 ✉ Southeast of Limassol
🍴 Tavernas on the beach

AMATHOUS

These interesting ruins, signposted as Amathounta Archaeological Park, are sprawled over a large area, and include a rock-cut tomb in the Amathus Beach Hotel grounds and an underwater site off the coast. Scramble about the remains of an agora, acropolis and Temple to Aphrodite in a fenced site off the main road.

➕ H8 ✉ 8km (5 miles) east of Limassol
🕐 Apr–end May, Sep–end Oct 8–6; Jun–end Aug 8–7.30; Nov–end Mar 8–5

🚌 Bus from Limassol and Larnaka
♿ None 💷 Inexpensive

AVDIMOU BEACH

This long sandy beach is one of the south's most attractive and the lack of crowds for much of the year, is what makes it so appealing. Weekends in summer are another story of course.

➕ E8 ✉ 3km (2 miles) off the main road
🍴 Tavernas on the beach

CYPRUS WINE MUSEUM

www.cypruswinemuseum.com

Cyprus was one of the first wine producing countries and this small but absorbing museum, in a traditional stone house, provides an excellent introduction to the country's wine history, via a guided visit, informative displays and wine tasting at the end.

➕ F8 ✉ 42 Odos Paphou, Erimi Village
☎ 2587 3808 🕐 Daily 9–5 ♿ Few
💷 Moderate

GOVERNOR'S BEACH

Backed by low white cliffs, this sheltered beach is one of Cyprus'

Remains of the ruined city of Amathous

A cat at home within St. Nicholas of the Cats monastery, Akrotiri Peninsula

loveliest and, fortunately, one of its most low-key. Swimming here is a delight due to the relatively calm sea. Tavernas overlook the sands and you can rent sunbeds and umbrellas.
➕ J8 ✉ Junction 16, Nicosia–Limassol motorway 🍴 Beachfront tavernas
♿ None

LEFKARA

Lefkara became famous for its lace, known as *lefkaritika*, in 1481 when Leonardo da Vinci is said to have ordered some for Milan's cathedral. Just as any fashion trend starts, soon after the Venetians were wanting it too, and so the industry of lace-making took off. Most of the lace shops line the hilly narrow streets of the upper town Pano Lefkara, although there are some in Kato Lefkara, the lower town, too. It gets crowded, and the old ladies can be aggressive sales women, but the town is lovely to wander around.
➕ J7 ✉ Junction 13, Nicosia–Limassol motorway 🍴 Restaurants and cafés
♿ None

LIMASSOL: ARCHAEOLOGICAL MUSEUM

A must-do for completists and a fine escape from the afternoon sun, this good little archaeological museum features finds from the Limassol area, from the 9th millennium BC to the late Roman period.
➕ G8 ✉ Corner of Odos Kanningos and Vyronos ☎ 2530 5157 🕐 Tue–Fri 8–3, Thu 8–5, Sat 9–3 🍴 Restaurants and cafés nearby ♿ Few 💵 Inexpensive

LIMASSOL: CASTLE AND MEDIEVAL MUSEUM

While the chapel where Richard the Lionheart married Berengaria is no longer standing, Limassol's medieval castle holds the engaging medieval collection of Nicosia's Cyprus Museum. Fascinating exhibits include armour, ceramics, bronze lamps and marble carvings.
➕ G8 ✉ Odos Eirinis in the old town, near the old harbour ☎ 2530 5419 🕐 Tue–Sat 9–5, Sun 10–1 🍴 Restaurants and cafés surrounding castle ♿ Few 💵 Moderate

★

The medieval castle, inland from Limassol's old harbour, which houses a museum

Locally made lace hanging outside a craftworker's house, Lefkara

Around Limassol

Limassol is best experienced with a stroll through its old quarter and bustling shopping area, absorbing the city's history on the way.

DISTANCE: 2.5km (1.5 miles) **ALLOW:** 3 hours with stops

START .... **END**

SEAFRONT SCULPTURE PARK   **SEAFRONT SCULPTURE PARK**

✚ G8

① Start in the morning or early evening. From the waterfront park, stroll the oceanside promenade to enjoy sea views, people-watching opportunities and striking sculptures.

② Follow the promenade to the roundabout with the old harbour to your left and old town on your right. Cross over to the old town and walk to the medieval museum (▷ 41).

③ Have a coffee in one of the numerous stylish cafés around the museum and enjoy this lively yet laidback quarter of the city.

④ Turn right into Odos Genthiliou Mitella, passing Al Kebir (big) Mosque, which is really not that big, to explore what was once the Turkish neighbourhood.

⑧ After your museum visit, stroll through the gardens, and across the road to the seafront where you can reward yourself with an ice cream or something cold.

⑦ Continue along Odos Agiou Andreou until you reach the northern side of the Municipal Gardens, then turn right on Odos Kanningkos to visit the Archaeological Museum (▷ 41), 200m (220 yards) to the left.

⑥ Continue for about 1km (0.62 miles), browsing the shops along the way and exploring the narrow lanes leading off, until you reach Odos Agias Trias. Take a detour here to admire the Agia Trias Church.

⑤ Continue northeast through this atmospheric quarter to Odos Agiou Andreou, Limassol's lovely main street.

THE SOUTHWEST

WALK

Limassol to Pafos

Drive past olive groves punctuated by green fields skirted by turquoise sea, to visit archaeological ruins and historical sites.

DISTANCE: 97km (60 miles)   **ALLOW:** 5 hours with stops

START

LIMASSOL

✚ G8

1 Start out early, drive west from Limassol (▷ 38) toward the new port and Asomatos and Fasouri, passing between tall pine trees and dense citrus groves.

2 At the sign for Kolossi Castle (▷ 36) turn north to visit this splendid outpost of the Knights Hospitallers. After Kolossi village turn left and continue to Episkopi village.

3 Founded in the 7th century by refugees from Kourion, Episkopi is now home to British forces. Stop at nearby Kourion (▷ 37) to visit the archaeological site.

4 Continue west in the direction of Pafos for Kourion's stadium and a further 2km (1.25 miles) for the Temple of Apollo Ylatis, another set of interesting ruins.

END

PAFOS

✚ C8

8 Cruise into Pafos (▷ 53) to refuel at a waterfront restaurant before exploring the sights.

7 Continue driving west for another 6km (3.5 miles) to Petra tou Romiou (▷ 39), the mythical birthplace of Aphrodite. Heading northwest, take the turning to Kouklia village and the archaeological site of Palaiapafos, where Aphrodite was worshipped.

6 Turn off left to admire Avidmou Beach (▷ 40), around 3km (2 miles) away. A few kilometers further and you can stop at Pissouri to take a stroll along the beach before heading up to the village.

5 Drive through the British services' base and sports fields of Happy Valley.

DRIVE

Shopping

BAGS OF FUN

Fans of vintage clothes and accessories could lose themselves in this gem of a store for hours—better let your other-half know where you're going before you leave the hotel. Expect to find beautiful antique and retro jewellery, accessories and fashion.

G8 ✉ 44 Odos Elados, Limassol ☎ 2576 2575

CALIA MONOYIOU ALTA MODA

www.monoyiou.com
This Cyprus-born designer showcases the dramatic yet playful style of Greek fashion with bright colours and ample use of sequins. Her wedding gowns are very much sought after by the upper echelons of the Cypriot social scene.

G8 ✉ 6a Ayias Zonis ☎ 2535 9496

COSTAS THEODOROU

www.costastheodorou.com.cy
Cypriots swear by the fine quality of the leather goods produced by this Cypriot maker. The handbags, purses and travelling bags are all beautifully made. They also stock international brands but go for the local stuff.

G8 ✉ 129 Odos Anexartisias, Limassol ☎ 2536 8031

CYPRUS HANDICRAFT SERVICE

Sponsored by the Ministry of Commerce, Industry and Tourism, this reputable handicrafts shop (one of only four in total) is the place to head for traditional souvenirs, ranging from silverware to embroidery. The workmanship is excellent and you can be certain you're getting an original, not a fake.

G8 ✉ 25 Odos Themidos, Limassol ☎ 2530 5118

PANA'S PATCHWORK CREATION

www.panas-creations.com
The handmade gifts here won't be to everyone's taste but there are some beautiful things, such as lovingly made patchwork quilts, cushion covers and footstools. But then there's kitschy stuff too, including covered tissue box holders and jewellery boxes.

G8 ✉ 21 Odos Saripolou, Limassol ☎ 2536 3642

QUALITY LEATHER

Cyprus is known for its fine quality leather—it's amazingly soft and smells beautiful. You'll see leather shops all over the island, especially in Limassol and Pafos, but the problem is that most of the styles are outdated. If you can't find anything you like, ask if they make to order; most do. But it's best to take a similar item or photograph of something you like to show them.

PRECIOUS METAL GALLERY

If you prefer one-of-a-kind contemporary pieces when it comes to jewellery, then put this shop at the top of your list. Evis Michaelides creates silver and gold jewellery in imaginative shapes and forms using the art of cloisonné enamelling, which is said to have originated in Cyprus.

G8 ✉ Shop 17, Agora Anexartisias, Odos Anexartisias, Limassol ☎ 2535 3639

SEA SPONGE EXHIBITION CENTRE

www.apacy.com
It's hard to overlook this big dusty store, which seems to have been here forever, with its baskets of seashells and starfish and displays of fake fish and other sea creatures in the window. The sea sponges are the thing to buy, as they make good gifts for loved ones back home, squishing up nice and small.

G8 ✉ Old Port, Limassol ☎ 2587 1656

STRATIS LEATHERLAND

This is one of the few leather stores to stock contemporary pieces alongside classic shapes that never go out of fashion. If you can't find what you want they also make to order.

G8 ✉ 132 Odos Agiou Andreou, Limassol ☎ 2536 3061

ANTITHESIS

www.thesis.com.cy
Adjoining the stylish Thesis interiors, furniture and design store, this hip little café does excellent coffees to a smooth jazz soundtrack and there's a bookstore and magazines to thumb through.

➕ G8 ✉ 207 Odos Agiou Andreou, Limassol
☎ 2536 9765

BREEZE

Right on the beach, this alfresco bar is the place to head if you like to hear the sound of the sea and feel the breeze in your face while sipping an icy-cold something. All ages and types are here by day, but by night it's usually a young and beautiful crowd. Not far from here, Pebbles is a similar place.

➕ G8 ✉ 90 Georgiou I, Limassol ☎ 2532 1294

CATAMARAN CRUISE

www.interyachting.com.cy
Join a relaxing full-day cruise (with swimming) on a catamaran either from Paphos to the Akamas Peninsula via Coral Bay and Lara, or from Limassol Old Port to Cape Gata. Buffet lunch and drinks are served and transfers are included. Also sunset sailing.

➕ G8/C8/C6 ✉ Limassol, Paphos and Latchi Harbour
☎ 2581 1900

DRAUGHT

www.carobmill-restaurants.com
Cyprus' first microbrewery

pours tasty ales that they'll let you try for free. Open all day, it gets crowded late with locals. The buzzy atmosphere is great, especially when there's a DJ playing.

➕ G8 ✉ Carob Mill, Odos Vasilissis, Limassol
☎ 2582 0470

FASOURI WATERMANIA WATERPARK

www.fasouri-watermania.com
This waterpark (voted one of Europe's top three in 2007) is a great place to bring the kids. Or kids at heart. There are lots of waterslides, a wave pool, water rides and a lazy river, along with sunbeds and umbrellas, eateries and gift shop.

➕ F8–G8 ✉ Lanitis Orange Groves, Fasouri ☎ 2571 4235

FLO CAFÉ

This super-stylish branch

GREEN GOLF?

For an island whose dams were running at 5.4 per cent capacity in August 2008, the expansion of golf tourism on Cyprus appears to be madness brought on by the summer sun. But still the government insists on giving permits for new courses and clubs (mainly because of the island's stagnating tourism growth), while in the meantime negotiating with Lebanon to import water if the crisis gets worse.

of the Greek café chain has one of Cyprus' best sun terraces overlooking the ocean and within splashing distance of the sea. Great coffee, iced frappes and icy cold beers, but the views are what they do best.

➕ G8 ✉ 106 Georgiou I (near the Londa hotel), Limassol ☎ 2587 9610

RIALTO THEATRE

www.rialto.com.cy
This beautifully renovated art deco theatre plays host to world-class theatre, modern dance, classical music and ballet, and music, dance and film festivals—anything from the Cyprus Symphony Orchestra to the Bolshoi Ballet.

➕ G8 ✉ 19 Odos Andrea Drousioti, Heroes Square, Limassol ☎ 2534 3900

VIKLA GOLF AND COUNTRY CLUB

www.vikla-golf.com
Locals love this par 72 family-owned golf club because the fees are low, the countryside is gorgeous and the facilities are great, but most of all because it's eco-friendly. Like most Cypriots they are conscious of water use, so they rely on rain for the winter and let the greens brown off in summer.

➕ H7 ✉ Vikla-Kellaki Village, 30 minutes from Limassol
☎ 9967 4218

Restaurants

APOLLO TAVERNA (€)

www.columbia-hotels.com
You can expect good portions by day at this elegant traditional taverna, but head here at night and you had better be prepared for a long multi-course 'Apollon Meze'. Go with an empty stomach—it's worth it!

🚩 E9 ✉ Columbia Beach Resort, Pissouri Bay ☎ 2583 3000 🕐 Daily lunch, dinner

ARTIMA (€)

www.carobmill-restaurants.com
This big, stylish Italian restaurant is the place for lunch or dinner. By day it's popular with local workers and business-people, while evenings see couples and groups of friends lingering over a slow meal.

🚩 G8 ✉ Carob Mill complex, Odos Vasilissis, Limassol ☎ 2582 0466 🕐 Daily lunch, dinner

BEIGE (€€)

The food at Beige can be hit and miss, but when it's good, it's very good. Expect an eclectic menu featuring international, Cypriot and even Japanese cuisine, in a big beautiful dimly lit space.

🚩 G8 ✉ 238 Odos Agiou Andreou, Limassol ☎ 2581 8860 🕐 Mon–Sat dinner only

CAPRICE (€€)

www.londahotel.com
The chic Londa hotel's Italian restaurant is one of Cyprus' best, dishing up classic Italian and Mediterranean cuisine with a twist. The restaurant itself is gorgeous, and features a good wine list and excellent staff.

🚩 G8 ✉ Londa Hotel, 72 Georgiou I, Limassol ☎ 2586 5555 🕐 Daily dinner only

DIONYSOS (€€€)

www.columbia-hotels.com
Considered to be one of the finest restaurants on the island, expect creative cuisine making use

of quality ingredients and exquisitely presented. Service is attentive.

🚩 E9 ✉ Columbia Beach Resort, Pissouri Bay ☎ 2583 3000 🕐 Varies according to season

FLAVOURS OF INDIA (€)

www.flavoursofindia.eu
If you're looking for a break from Cypriot cuisine or simply craving a curry, head to this down-to-earth eatery for authentic Indian.

🚩 E9 ✉ Shop 1–2 Ambelonon, Pissouri Bay ☎ 2522 2681 🕐 Daily dinner only

MAVROMMATIS (€€€)

www.fourseasons.com.cy
At one of the most interesting restaurants in Cyprus, expect gastronomic Greek based on French technique. Each dish will impress, as will the outstanding wine list.

🚩 G8 ✉ Four Seasons hotel, Leoforos Amathus, Limassol ☎ 2585 8000 🕐 Daily dinner only

VIVALDI (€€€)

www.fourseasons.com.cy
Serving innovative and refined takes on Italian dishes, Vivaldi is Cyprus' finest restaurant. The service is exemplary and the wine list is excellent. Save it for your last night or a special occasion.

🚩 G8 ✉ Four Seasons hotel, Leoforos Amathus, Limassol ☎ 2585 8000 🕐 Tue–Sun dinner only

The West

Apart from Pafos's (Paphos's) pretty harbour and outstanding ruins, this is really the wild west. The Akamas Peninsula has wonderful wild flowers and the Baths of Aphrodite, while a drive to Lara reveals beaches in splendid isolation—apart from the march of the turtles through the sand.

4

5

Pomos Point

Pomos

Gialia

Chrysochou Bay

■ Argaka

Cape Arnaoutis
(Akamas)

**Lakki
(Latchi)**

Polis

Pelathousa

Neo
Chorio

Chrysochou ■

■ Steni

Lysos

6

Drouseia ■

■ Filousa

Sarama

Akourdaleia ■

Ineia ■

Kritou
Tera

Anadiou

Simou ■

Fyti

Lara

Giolou ■

Kannavi

Cape
Drepano

Kathikas ■

Theletra ■

Agios
Dimitrianos ■

**Agios
Georgios**

683
▲

■ Polemi

Pegeia ■

Stroumpi ■

Cho

7

■ Koili

*Coral
Bay*

**Agios
Neofytos
Monastery**

Letymvou ■

■ Kallepeia

Tsada ■

Kissonerga ■

Empa ■

■ Mesogi

Axylo

■ Anavargos

Episkopi

Pafos (Paphos)
District Archaeological Museum,
Ethnographic Museum

N

**Archaeological
Park**

**Geroskipou
Folk Art
Museum**

Foinik

Pafos ✈

A6

■ Anarita

8

Ko

**Sanctuary of
Aphrodite**

0 ——————— 10 km

0 ————— 5 miles

B   **C**

kkina
nköy)

Panagia
Chrysorrogiatissa
Monastery

gios
tios

Peravasa

Aglos
Ioannis

Arminou

Mandria

Pentalia

Omodos

Mesana

Arsos

argeti

Gerovasa

Kelokedara 771

Malia

Trachypedoula

eros

Stavrokonnou

Diarizos

Dora

Mamonia

Chapotami

leia

E   F

Akamas Peninsula

Walkers step out (left); the peninsula's varying scenery (right and opposite)

THE BASICS

🞢 B6
✉ West of Latchi, in the Polis area
🍴 Baths of Aphrodite Tourist Pavilion café
♿ Few
❓ Information signage in car park; get the free *Nature Trails of the Akamas* booklet from tourist offices

HIGHLIGHTS

● Walking trails, such as the Aphrodite Trail (7.5km/4.5 miles) and Adonis Trail (7.5km/4.5 miles)
● Baths of Aphrodite—where the goddess of love bathed
● Wild flowers and wonderful sea vistas

This breathtaking area is quintessentially Mediterranean with craggy hills strewn with limestone rocks, olive trees, pine and juniper, goats clambering about among the foliage, and a dramatic rocky coastline of coves and cobalt-coloured sea.

Unspoilt gem The Akamas Peninsula is a protected area on the westernmost extremity, unique in the south, not only for its beauty, but also for the absence of development. With a number of well-marked nature trails affording spectacular vistas of the coastline and sea all the way, and a rich and varied flora and wildlife, it's a paradise for walkers.

Flora The vegetation is typically Mediterranean, with impenetrable maquis interspersed with a thin covering of pine trees and wildflowers blanketing the hills, including cyclamen in autumn. In some places the landscape is stark with spectacular limestone outcrops and rock spilling down the hillside into the turquoise sea to create a dramatic picture.

Take a walk Signposted walking trails start near the Baths of Aphrodite, west of Latchi; there are information panels at the car park. The ascent to Moutti tis Sotiras along the circular 3-hour Aphrodite Trail is rewarded with magnificent views.

Jump on board Cruises on catamarans leave from Latchi, which sail along the coast stopping for swimming in the coves around Fontana Amoroza (Love's Spring) on the way to Cape Arnaoutis.

Lara

The sands of Lara Bay provide a safe birth-place for hard-to-see loggerhead turtles

THE BASICS

+ B6
✉ 26km (16 miles) north of Pafos
🍴 Saint George (▷ 64)
♿ None

HIGHLIGHTS

● Lara Beach, a long stretch of creamy sand
● Picturesque Lara Bay
● Wild walking trails leading down to sandy coves
● Loggerhead turtles, although you'll be lucky to see them

TIP

● If walking Lara peninsula, take bottles of water and snacks as there's nowhere to buy anything after you pass the tavernas near the car park.

The desolate headland of Lara, a wild and remote area of sandy beaches where the land sweeps up to the high hills and loggerhead turtles come ashore to breed, is one of Cyprus' most alluring spots.

Beautiful scenery This splendid, ecologically important coastal area centering on the windswept headland of Lara—home to a loggerhead turtle breeding centre, curvaceous Lara Bay and two long stretches of creamy sand beaches—is one of Cyprus' most attractive. Like the Akamas Peninsula, which it meets up with further north, Lara boasts a number of walking trails running along the coast, eventually joining those on the Akamas. Thicket, thorn and mimosa border the tracks and you can wander down narrow trails (by foot only) to the rocky shore and sandy coves. Unfortunately the hope of seeing any turtles is slim, depending on the cycle of the breeding season—nevertheless this is a wonderful place to explore.

Starting point The area is best approached from Agios Georgios, once a small village with little more than a church overlooking a fishing harbour, now surrounded by a sprawling development of villas and apartments. A reasonably well-graded dirt road hugs the coast for some 8km (5 miles), so it's possible to drive as far as the Lara headland, park the car and walk, or you can leave your car in the car park at Agios Georgios if you prefer. The road continues up the coast to Koppos Island, where it becomes somewhat rougher, and then on to the distant northwest Cape Arnaoutis in the Akamas.

TOP 25

Pafos

Pafos (Paphos) is a perplexing mix of tourism gone wild fused with compelling archaeological sites, such as the Tomb of the Kings, photogenic vistas, a lovely old habour and a medieval castle.

Historic Pafos The first settlement of Pafos dates from the 4th century BC, and just as Pafos played an important role in early Cypriot history, it's played a crucial role in the recent development of Cyprus' economy, as a popular tourism destination. After the Roman mosaics, Pafos' next most compelling attraction is the Tombs of the Kings, dating to the 3rd century BC. Some 100 tombs sprawl across a large rocky area, dotted with wild flowers in spring, and overlooking the sea. Steps lead down into the tombs and then into a series of spooky underground passageways and chambers.

Pafos today Modern Pafos is split into two, upper and lower, also known as Kitma and Kato Pafos. The upper town is where you will find the main commercial centre, shops and modern museums while the lower town contains most of the city's archaeological remains (▷ 54). The harbour is the focus of the lower town and is a lovely place to stroll and have a drink while watching the fishermen, the yachts and the local pelicans all do their thing. The harbour was originally guarded by two castles that were built by the Lusignans in the 13th century; both were badly damaged when the Ottomans attacked in 1570. One was restored and is now known as the Pafos Fort—access is across a drawbridge.

THE BASICS

➕ C8

🍴 Restaurants and cafés throughout town, especially on the harbour

♿ Few

✋ Tombs of the Kings moderate; Pafos Fort inexpensive; St. Paul's Pillar free

ℹ️ 3 Odos Gladstonos, tel 2693 2841; www.visitpafos.org.cy

HIGHLIGHTS

● The splendidly situated Tombs of the Kings
● Pafos old harbour and its waterside cafés
● The Pafos Fort, dungeons and drawbridge
● St. Paul's Pillar and the ruins of Agia Kyriaki
● The 2nd-century limestone Odeon with 11 rows of seats

Pafos:
Archaeological Park

HIGHLIGHTS

HIGHLIGHTS

- House of Dionysos–Ganymede being taken to Olympus by an eagle
- House of Aion–Leda and the Swan
- House of Theseus–Theseus killing the minotaur
- House of the Four Seasons–vivid hunting scenes

TIP

- Wear a hat and take a bottle of water with you as it can be scorching at this sprawling park and there's little shade.

This World Heritage-listed archaeological park features impressive, well-preserved Roman mosaics, atmospheric Byzantine castle ruins and a diminutive Odeon, all in a stunning seaside location.

The mosaics Adjacent to the relaxing harbour of Pafos, the beautiful mosaics on this site were found in five large 3rd-century villas that probably belonged to Roman noblemen. The House of Dionysos was excavated first, after a passing shepherd turned up some mosaic fragments. The most famous mosaic is that of the triumph of Dionysos as he heads across the skies in a chariot drawn by leopards. The House of Aion displays a very fine series of mosaics from the late 4th century, which were discovered in 1983. The House of Orpheus contains representations of Amazons, Hercules

The remains of a ruined medieval fort at Saranta Kolones, Pafos (left); detail of mosaic floors discovered in the House of Dionysos and other buildings of the Roman period (right, top and bottom)

and the Lion of Nemea, alongside very impressive mosaics featuring Orpheus surrounded by animals who, oddly enough, appear to be listening to his music. The main mosaic in the House of Theseus is that of Theseus killing the minotaur, although there are some others featuring Achilles and Neptune. The House of the Four Seasons, unearthed in 1992, boasts the most beautiful mosaics showing the God of the Seasons and a variety of hunting scenes.

Other highlights The crumbling Byzantine Fortress of Saranta Kolones (Forty Columns) dates from around the 7th century, though it was rebuilt in the 12th century. The partially restored Odeon, below the lighthouse, was built in the 2nd century AD, during the Roman period, but suffered earthquake damage in the 7th century.

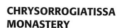

More to See

AGIOS GEORGIOS

Agios Georgios is home to a splendid sandstone Greek-Cypriot orthodox church of the same name. A pretty fishing harbour, stunning views north along the coast and the west coast's best seafood restaurant, Saint George, all contribute to making Agios Georgios worth a visit.

🕂 B7 ✉ 25km (15 miles) north of Pafos 🍴 Saint George (▷ 64) ♿ Few

AGIOS NEOFYTOS MONASTERY

The Cypriot hermit and writer Saint Neofytos carved these fascinating caves out of the mountains and lived here in the 12th century, creating the three chambers that are decorated with fine Byzantine frescoes, dating from the 12th to 15th century. In the monastery's church there are also some exquisite icons from the 16th century post-Byzantine period.

🕂 C7 ✉ Village of Tala, 10km (6 miles) north of Pafos 🕐 Apr–end Oct 9–1, 2–4; Nov–end Mar 9–4 🍴 Café nearby 🚌 Limited buses from Pafos ♿ None 🖐 Inexpensive

CHRYSORROGIATISSA MONASTERY

Dating to 1770 (although originally founded in the 12th century) and perched precariously on the edge of a mountain at a height of 610m (2,000ft), 'Our Lady of the Golden Pomegranate' Monastery is worth visiting for its stunning location and spectacular valley views. Inside, there's an ornate church, a small treasury museum with exquisite icons, and the Abbot paints his own icons and makes some very good wine, both for sale.

🕂 D7 ✉ 3km (1.5 miles) south of Panagia, 40km (25 miles) from Pafos ☎ 2672 2457 🕐 Sep–end Apr daily 10–12.30, 1.30–4; May–end Aug 9.30–12.30, 1.30–6.30 ♿ Few 🖐 Free; donation welcome

GEROSKIPOU FOLK ART MUSEUM

This splendid museum, housed in an 18th-century stone house, features fascinating displays of traditional costumes, musical instruments, furnishings, crafts and folk art from the 19th

Agios Neofytos Monastery (above); Chrysorrogiatissa Monastery (opposite)

and 20th century. Woodwork, metal-work, pottery, embroidery, spinning, weaving, and the production of silk, hemp, flax and rope are represented. Some rooms are set up as they were at the time with their everyday objects, including a 'pastos' room where wedding festivities were held.

✚ C8 ✉ Geroskipou, 3km (2 miles) east of Pafos, on the airport road ☎ 2630 6216 🕐 Apr–end Oct daily 9–5; Nov–end Mar 8–4 🍴 Café on the corner ♿ Few ♨ Inexpensive

LATCHI

Although rapidly developing into a major tourist resort, Latchi (Lakki) is nevertheless a charming beachside hamlet, with a handful of excellent seafood restaurants on the harbour and a long sandy beach backed by tavernas. There are few things lovelier than lingering over a long lunch of seafood on a Sunday with the boats bobbing in the marina beside you.

✚ C6 ✉ 5km (3 miles) west of Polis 🍴 Numerous restaurants and cafés ♿ Good

OMODOS

This pretty village of cobblestone lanes and stone houses on the lower slopes of the Troodos has lots of character and charm. There's very little to do except browse the traditional craft shops or sit back with a drink at a delightful café, but nobody seems to mind.

✚ F7 ✉ 32km (20 miles) northeast of Pafos 🍴 Several tavernas and cafés

PAFOS: DISTRICT ARCHAEOLOGICAL MUSEUM

Home to a wealth of archaeological treasures unearthed at sites in the Pafos region, from prehistoric through to classical times, this museum is definitely worth an hour of your time. There are just five exhibition rooms along with relics in a yard. Look out for the clay vessels that were moulded onto the body for therapeutic purposes.

✚ C8 ✉ Leoforous Georgiou Griva Digeni Drive ☎ 2630 6215 🕐 Tue, Wed, Fri 8–3, Thu 8–5, Sat 9–3 🍴 Cafés nearby ♿ Few ♨ Inexpensive

Looking across the harbour at Latchi

The renovated monastery at Omodos

PAFOS: ETHNOGRAPHIC MUSEUM

Equally as fascinating as Pafos' Archaeological Museum, is this small museum housing the private collection of local professor George Eliades. There are some lovely traditional costumes, among many other intriguing everyday objects from Cypriot life.

➕ C8 ✉ 1 Odos Exo Vrisis ☎ 2693 2010 🕐 Mon–Sat 9.30–5, Sun 10–1 🍴 Cafés nearby ♿ Few ✋ Inexpensive

PANAGIA

The birthplace of the Greek-Cypriots' beloved first president, Archbishop Makarios—a key player in the move toward independence. The Cultural Centre has exhibits of his memorabilia and around the corner is his home.

➕ D7 ✉ Pano Panagia village centre ☎ 2672 2473 or 2672 2255 🕐 May–end Sep 9–1, 3-6; Oct–end Apr 9–1, 2–4 🍴 Café nearby ♿ Few ✋ Inexpensive

POMOS

One of Cyprus' loveliest spots, more so for the low-key charm of the place and lack of development than for any extraordinary beauty; although there are some pristine sandy beaches, pretty coves and attractive fishing harbours. As the road rises to giddy heights beyond Pomos Point there are breathtaking vistas over the coast.

➕ D5 ✉ 22km (13 miles) northwest of Polis 🍴 Tavernas and cafes along the coast

SANCTUARY OF APHRODITE

The ruins of the Sanctuary of Aphrodite at Palaiapafos in Kouklia village, testify to Aphrodite's importance. Rituals occurred where the Roman-era ruins lie, while inside the museum an enormous black stone, considered to be a manifestation of Aphrodite, was worshipped by pilgrims. The museum's other highlights include Roman glassware that dates from 58–395AD and a marble and stone sarcophagus supported on lion's legs and depicting scenes from Homeric epics.

➕ D8 ✉ 14km (8 miles) east of Pafos ☎ 2693 4250 🕐 Mon–Sat 10–4 ♿ Few ✋ Moderate

A shepherd tends his flock in the arid pastures near Pomos

Ruins of the Sanctuary of Aphrodite

Pafos to Latchi

With its beautiful coastline, this is a rewarding area to explore, whether you're a beachcomber, bird-lover or turtle-spotter.

DISTANCE: 195km (122 miles)   **ALLOW:** 6–8 hours including stops

START ·······················   ······················· **END**

PAFOS   **LATCHI**
➕ C8   ➕ C6

① From Pafos (▷ 53), drive north, following signs for Polis. Take the left turn for Coral Bay. Appreciate the bays and beaches, still attractive despite the development.

② Stop for a coffee at a café, before heading north to Agios Georgios (▷ 56). Head down to the fishing harbour to enjoy the boats and views along the coast.

③ Back at the car park follow the signs for Lara (▷ 52). The graded gravel road is manageable by car until you reach the beautiful Lara headland.

④ Get out and breathe in the sea air. From Lara, backtrack to Agios Georgios; the road onward is best by 4WD. Take the high road to Pegeia, north through citrus orchards to Polis.

⑧ Once at Polis, continue west through town to Latchi (▷ 58) harbour and reward yourself with a seafood supper by the sea before heading back to Pafos.

⑦ Stop at Kato Pyrgos for a coffee at a traditional coffee shop, then return and enjoy this lovely stretch all over again.

⑥ Drive east along the coastal road, passing sandy beaches, beautiful coves and fishing harbours along the way. From laidback Pomos (▷ 59) the winding road climbs, taking you through gorgeous pine-covered green mountains dotted with goats.

⑤ Wander around Polis' tiny old centre. Refuel at an alfresco café.

Shopping

ATHOS DIAMONDS
www.athos.com.cy
Popping the question or perhaps celebrating an anniversary or special occasion, and you want to buy a very special souvenir, then head here for diamonds, precious gems and exquisite jewellery. This is where the Cypriots shop and certification is provided so you know you're getting the real thing.
➕ C8 ✉ Shop 80, Lighthouse, Leoforos Poseidonos, Pafos
☎ 2681 1630

THE BEACH HUT
Some great beach and surfwear here including Ripcurl and Scorpion Bay. The shop also stocks one of a kind designs by the owners. You can kit yourself out for a laid back holiday at this store.
➕ C8 ✉ 31 Tomb of the Kings Road, Paphos
☎ 9996 7666

COSTAS THEODOROU
www.costastheodorou.com.cy
Considered by locals to be the best purveyor of fine quality leatherwear and accessories, this is the place to come for the softest coats and jackets, and beautiful bags, purses and belts.
➕ C8 ✉ 92 Leoforos Makarios, Pafos ☎ 2693 8390

CYPRUS HANDICRAFT SERVICE
The best place to buy traditional souvenirs on the island of Cyprus is at this government-sponsored handicrafts centre. Not only is the quality of workmanship excellent, but you're guaranteed it's an original handmade item. Expect to find anything and everything Cypriot here, from colourful woven textiles and simple rustic rugs, to olive wood carvings and wooden bowls and spoons. If you don't have time to visit Lefkara, they also stock Lefkara lace.
➕ C8 ✉ 64 Leoforos Apostolou Pavlou, Pafos
☎ 2630 6243

KIVOTOS
www.kivotosgallery.com
Kivotos brings together renowned Cypriot and Greek craftspeople selling ceramics, glass, sculptures, jewellery and wall hangings made in their own unique styles. A history of the techniques and materials used in each piece is on hand for your information.
➕ C8 ✉ 67 Odos Agoras, Pafos ☎ 2694 6075

KYKLOS GALLERY
Souvenirs don't come more original than this. This wonderful commercial gallery specializes in selling fine local Cypriot art, and the prices are very reasonable.
➕ C8 ✉ 6 Odos Minoos, Kato Pafos ☎ 2693 6681

LEMBA POTTERY
www.lembapottery.com
Lemba village has evolved into an artists' community in recent years and is home to an art school. However, it's the town's beautiful pottery that is getting the attention. All items at the Lemba Pottery are handmade and original.
➕ C8 ✉ 18 Odos Eleftherias, Lemba village ☎ 2627 0822

MOUFFLON BOOKSHOP
www.moufflonpaphos.com
Head to this Pafos branch of Cyprus' best bookshop for your holiday reading no other store has such a comprehensive English language section and as wide a range of books on Cypriot history, politics and culture, along with gorgeous coffee table books, too.
➕ C8 ✉ 30 Kinyras, Pafos
☎ 2693 4850

GOING POTTY

It should be no surprise that Cyprus is known for its pottery–after all, the Cypriots have been making pottery for thousands of years and were known for their decorative flair. Today, while giant jugs (*pitharia*) for storing wine are not needed, vases, pots, jars, plates and bowls, as well as purely decorative pieces, are still handmade, fired and decorated. Styles vary from the earthy look in the *pitharia* style to bright painted pieces. Go to Lemba village for the best work.

Entertainment and Activities

BARRIO DEL MAR

www.barriodelmar.com

This alfresco beachside club is the place to be if dancing on the sand within splashing distance of the sea—until the sun rises—is your idea of summer fun. There are appearances from regular guest DJs from around the globe, bongo drummers and dancers.

➕ C8 ✉ Geroskipou Beach, Geroskipou ☎ 9963 2229 ⏰ Summer 11.30pm–late

CAFÉ LA PLACE ROYALE

A favourite café with Cypriots, expats and tourists who like to linger over coffee or a cocktail on the shady alfresco terrace out front, which must provide some of the best people-watching opportunities in Pafos.

➕ C8 ✉ 1 Leoforos Poseidonos, Pafos ☎ 2693 3995

FREETIME TOURS

www.freetimetours.com

This company offers a range of guided and catered day tours by minibus or on 4x4 jeeps. Visit Kyrenia in the north, the capital Nicosia, explore the Troodos Mountains and the Akamas Peninsula, or visit traditional Cypriot villages in the hinterland. The team can also organise diving expeditions.

➕ C8 ✉ Polympian Complex shop 3, Danaes Avenue, Pafos ☎ 2681 3270

GEORGE'S JEEP SAFARI

George has a reputation for being the best of a bunch of tour operators offering 4WD-trips into the Akamas and Troodos, and he's also a lot of fun. Lunch is generally included along with a break for a swim.

➕ C8 ✉ 2 Marathos Avenue, Choraka ☎ 2627 1992

LOFT

There are so many bars, pubs and clubs on what is known as 'Bar Street' that it can be hard to decide which to go to. Loft is a longstanding favourite—a massive place, the DJ spins a combination of crowd-pleasing global dance hits all night long.

➕ C8 ✉ Bar Street, Pafos

MOUNTAIN CLIMBS

Over the past couple of years or so climbing routes have sprouted up all over Cyprus' mountains. There are now plenty of opportunities for climbing on the island and Nicosia and Pafos are particularly popular bases for expeditions. For more information on routes, visit the Cyprus Climbing and Mountaineering Federation (www.komoa. com) or for courses visit Mountain Sports & Rescue (www.cyprusclimbing.com).

☎ 9942 8143 ⏰ Summer Fri, Sat 11pm–late

PAPHOS SEA CRUISES

www.paphosseacruises.com

Hop on board these luxury cruisers or a lovely catamaran for a trip up to the Akamas peninsula. The boats leave from Pafos harbour, and lunch is included, along with swimming in a secluded cove somewhere.

➕ C8 ✉ Odos Apostolos Pavlos, Pafos ☎ 2691 0200

WHEELIE CYPRUS

www.wheeliecyprus.com

These mountain-bike trips and walking tours (for all ages and level of fitness) in the Polis area come highly recommended. Guided day rides include the bike hire, helmet, gloves, vehicle support and transfers. Alternatively, you can hire a bike for a day or week and they'll deliver it free to your door.

➕ C6 ✉ Polis area; pick up from your accommodation ☎ 9935 0898

ZEPHYROS ADVENTURE SPORTS

www.enjoycyprus.com

This highly respected local tour company offers every kind of adventure and water sport imaginable, including kayaking, canoeing, mountain biking, trekking, snorkelling and scuba-diving.

➕ C8 ✉ Shop 7 Byzantium Gardens, Pafos ☎ 2693 0037

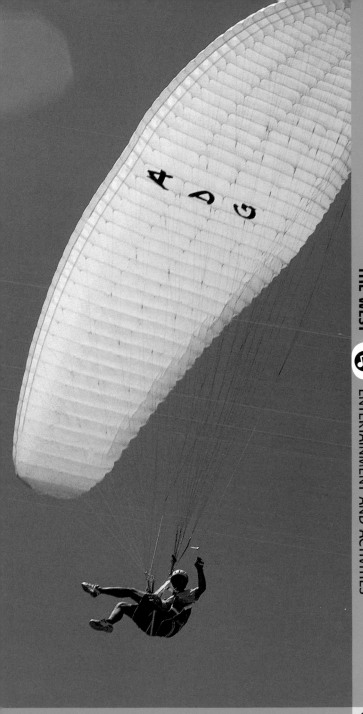

Restaurants

ARTIO BRASSERIE (€€)

www.artiobrasserie.com
This casual bistro serves light, international dishes; everything from big American-style salads to authentic Italian beef *carpaccio*. Its location near the Tombs of the Kings make it a good stop to head for an early dinner after a day exploring archaeological ruins.
🚲 C8 🖂 6 Pyramou, off Tombs of the Kings Road, Pafos ☎ 2694 2800 ⏱ Mon–Sat dinner only

CAVALLINI (€€)

While you'll find classic Italian dishes alongside slightly more creative, modern takes on old standards, the highlight for many is the tasty authentic pasta.
🚲 C8 🖂 Poseidonos 65, Pafos ☎ 2696 4164 ⏱ Daily dinner only

GINA'S PLACE (€)

www.ginasplacecyprus.com
Expats adore this casual café/bistro where you can tuck into delicious gourmet sandwiches, fresh salads and terrines, or a hearty pasta with a coffee or a glass of wine.

While the atmosphere is casual and friendly, everyone here takes food very seriously. There's a deli counter in the corner that makes it an ideal stop for your picnic supplies.
🚲 C8 🖂 Agiou Antoniou 3, Kato Pafos ☎ 2693 8017 ⏱ Mon–Sat 9.30–10

MANDRA TAVERN (€€)

www.mandra-tavern.com
This traditional taverna dishes up authentic Greek and Cypriot standards to loyal regulars who keep coming back for more.
🚲 C8 🖂 4 Dionysou, Kato Pafos ☎ 2693 4129 ⏱ Daily dinner only

O'SHIN SUSHI BAR (€€)

This stylish Japanese eatery provides what many consider to be the best sushi in Cyprus; an ideal choice if you've

been overdosing on Greek food.
🚲 C8 🖂 Elysium Hotel, Vasilissis Verenikis, Pafos ☎ 2684 4444 ⏱ Daily dinner only

SAINT GEORGE (€)

This is the kind of seafood restaurant where the aromas of freshly fried fish serve as a mouthwatering reminder that will have you wanting to return for more. With the freshest seafood on the coast, needless to say, the calamari and chips are memorable.
🚲 B7 🖂 Agios Georgios ☎ 2662 1306 ⏱ Daily until 6pm

SEVEN ST. GEORGES (€€)

www.7stgeorgestavern.com
Another expat favourite, this award-winning restaurant serves refined Greek dishes with a gourmet twist. The owner offers his own fine wines.
🚲 C8 🖂 Geroskipou, Pafos ☎ 2696 3176 ⏱ Daily lunch, dinner

YIANGOS & PETER (€)

There could be few better places to while away the time than sitting in the sun outside at this superb seafood taverna with the boats bobbing nearby in the harbour. The meze are delicious, the fried seafood is fantastic, and servings are generous.
🚲 C7 🖂 Latchi Harbour, Latchi, west of Polis ☎ 2632 1411 ⏱ Daily lunch, dinner

Nicosia (Lefkosia/Lefkoşa) is an intriguing city with a charming, yet ramshackle, old city and the peculiarity of being the world's only divided city. The High Troodos will have you winding through apple trees, olive groves and vineyards, before reaching the fresh pine air of Mount Olympos.

Agios Ioannis Cathedral,
Archbishop Makarios III Cultural Centre,
Cyprus Museum,
Famagusta Gate,
Hadjigeorgakis Kornesios House,
Laïki Geitonia,
Leventis Municipal Museum,
Old Walled City,
Omeriye Hamam,
Omeriye Mosque

**LEFKOSIA
(NICOSIA / LEFKOŞA)**

Deneia

Kokkinotrimithia

Aglantzia

eristerona

Akaki

Palaiometocho

Strovolos

Meniko

Kato
Lakatameia
Pano
Lakatameia

Geri

Orounta

Serrachis

Pano
Deftera

Kato
Deftera

Gialias

Agios
Sozomenos

Mitsero

Ergates

Psimolofou

Potamia

Politiko

Pera

Klirou

Margi

Pera
Chorio

Dali

Kampia

Pediaios

Alampra

Fikardou

Mathiatis

Sia

Gourri

**Machairas
Monastery**

Lythrodontas

Palaichori

silia

Kampl

Vavatsinia

Agioi Vavatsinas

opetra

Melini

rakapas Eptagoneia

H   J   K

Nicosia: Cyprus Museum

Examples of the statues and figurines found at the Cyprus Museum

THE BASICS

➕ a3
✉ 1 Leoforos Mouseiou
☎ 2286 5888 or 2286 5864
🕐 Tue–Sat 8–4 (Thu to 5pm), Sun 10–1
🍴 Café opposite museum
♿ Few
💷 Moderate

HIGHLIGHTS

● An anthropomorphic idol from Choirokoitia dating from between 7000–6000BC
● Nude female figurine from Lempa dating to 2500BC
● Beautiful head of a woman with decorative headdress from Arsos (480–450BC)
● 5th-century bronze lions viciously attacking a bull from Vouni

The island's most engaging museum, Nicosia's Cyprus Museum has a world-class collection of archaeological finds from important sites across the country. Stop here first to ensure you get a lot more out of your visits to other sites.

The collection The museum features a vast range of objects covering the development of civilization on the island from 8000BC to the early Christian period. It's a compact museum with quality displays and too few visitors, making it a must do for any lover of eras past. The museum's 14 rooms house most of the important finds from sites across Cyprus—from the Neolithic period through to the Chalcolithic, Bronze, Archaic, Classical, Hellenistic and Roman to the early Christian period. The thematic displays follow a chronological order, demonstrating the country's astonishingly lengthy historical journey.

Most noteworthy Highlights include striking Bronze Age figurines and vases, beautiful Mycenaean objects from Kourion, and sophisticated pottery and glassware. Two thousand clay figurines found at Agia Irini are displayed as they were originally found, gathered around a single altar. Room ten is devoted to the evolution of writing in Cyprus, from Cypro-Minoan script to Cypro-syllabic script, and finally the alphabetic script. There are also a wide range of sculptures on show, as well as a huge bronze statue of Emperor Septimius Severus and the famous green-horned god from Enkomi.

Statue of Archbishop Makarios (left); the city walls (middle) conceal old narrow streets (right)

Nicosia: Old Walled City

An imposing stone wall encircling the city and eleven stout bastions give Nicosia's (Lefkosia's/Lefkoşa's) old city its distinctive form. Despite gentrification in parts, the city has a charmingly dilapidated feel and is a delight to explore.

Defences Constructed by the Venetians, Nicosia's formidable ramparts remain substantially intact. Pafos Gate to the west is a little battered and Kyrenia Gate ruined, while Famagusta Gate, once the important eastern entrance into the city, is now a cultural centre that seems to be constantly closed for renovation. The enormous moat- always intended to be dry—that once provided a deep and formidable barrier to full-scale attack, is now a collection of gardens, car parks and football pitches. While the walls did an admirable job at keeping invaders at bay, the Ottomans managed to break through in 1570 after a siege of 70 days.

A better future Today, Ledra and Onasagorau streets in the southern sector are bustling shopping streets, while the renovated Laiki Geitonia quarter is popular with tourists. The northern side is just as lively. Despite renovations taking place in parts of the city, both sides still retain a ramshackle feel, with some buildings near the Green Line still scarred with bullet-holes. At the time of research, the Green Line still separated the north from the south, with barbed wire and guard boxes along the route, although the Ledra Street (Odos Lidras) barricade was pulled down in March 2008 and talks were underway that could see the city unified.

THE BASICS

➕ a2
✉ Centre of Nicosia
🍴 Taverns at Laiki Geitonia and cafés on Ledra Street
♿ Few
ℹ Odos Aristokyprou, Laiki Geitonia, tel 2267 4264

HIGHLIGHTS

● Ledra Street (Odos Lidras), a lively pedestrian shopping street
● Laïki Geitonia, a charming quarter of tavernas and tourist shops
● Myriad museums, mosques and churches
● The Green Line—walk it before it comes down

TIP

● Take care walking the old city at night as some streets are very dark with little lighting.

NICOSIA AND THE HIGH TROODOS ★ TOP 25

Troodos Mountains

Mount Olympos (left), the highest mountain in the Troodos Mountains (right)

THE BASICS

➕ F1

🍴 Taverna and cafés in villages

❓ Pick up a free map of the Troodos area from any Cyprus Tourism Organization office

HIGHLIGHTS

● Mount Olympos—at 1,952m (6,402ft), the highest point on the island
● Cedar Valley—over 200,000 cedars, a local variety related to the Lebanese ones
● Splendid monasteries such as Chrysorrogiatissa, Kykkos and Machairas
● Byzantine churches Panagia tou Araka and Stavros tou Agiasmati
● Walking trails that criss-cross the Troodos

Far removed from the resorts often seen as typically Cyprus, these mountains have twisting roads shaded by trees, wild flowers in spring and snow in winter, while the monasteries and villages make engaging stops along the way.

Flora The Troodos is an extensive area, running from west of Larnaka to the high ground of Mount Olympos then falling gradually to the western coast. Terraced vineyards shape the lower southern slopes with Aleppo pine covering the higher ground. The summits are covered in pine trees and spiky scrub, relieved occasionally with wild flowers. The northern slopes are different yet again, with dark poplar trees standing out in the valley alongside golden oak and rock rose. In the western Troodos the forest takes over and Cedar Valley is renowned for its magnificent giant cedars.

It's snowing In summer the high elevation makes for cooler temperatures so Cypriots enjoy taking a break from the heat, leaving the foreigners to bake down on the beaches. A big attraction in winter is the somewhat fickle snow, but when it does arrive (usually in January), everyone heads up the mountains for snowplay or to hit the relatively gentle slopes for some skiing on Mount Olympos (▷ 77).

Architecture The Troodos is also home to some splendid monasteries, boasting exquisite gold mosaics and icons, and small Byzantine churches featuring beautiful vivid frescoes.

Stunning frescoes adorn the inside of the charming, little stone church

Troodos Mountains: Asinou Church

Splendid Asinou Church in the Troodos Mountains has remained unscathed for 900 years and its beautiful old frescoes, some dating back to the 12th century, make it the best of Cyprus's many stunning painted churches.

World Heritage Site Perched atop a small mound beneath hills thick with eucalyptus and pine trees, the small church boasts a steep clay-tiled outer roof to protect its vulnerable Byzantine dome and treasures inside—so precious that UNESCO has included Our Lady of Asinou Church on the World Heritage list. The church is all that remains of the Monastery of Phorvia, founded in 1099, and some of the history of the monastery is contained within the stories told through the wall paintings. These frescoes comprise what is Cyprus's most beautiful church interior.

Paintings The single-aisle church dates from 1105, with additions from the 12th and 14th centuries. Mostly constructed from volcanic stone, only the door arches are made from brick, and while it was originally plastered, only fragments of the plaster remain. While the roof was originally wood, today it is covered with wood and tiles, dating from 1959. It's the dark interior that's of most importance; the most significant paintings date from 1105–1106. The *Communion of the Apostles,* found in the sanctuary apse, is a stunning example from this period. Later works appear in the nave, but of note is the *Forty Holy Martyrs of Sebaste*, dating from the earlier period.

THE BASICS

✚ G6

✉ Nikitari

☎ 9983 0329; if unattended phone Father Kyriakos Christofi Nikitari for the keys

🕐 Daily 9.30–1, 2–4

♿ Few

💷 Free; donation appreciated

❓ Excellent booklet on sale at the church

HIGHLIGHTS

● Scenes from the Second Coming
● *Communion of the Apostles*
● The Patronal scene
● *The Betrayal*, the *Way of the Cross*, the *Crucifixion*, and the *Entombment*
● The *Forty Holy Martyrs of Sebaste*

Troodos Mountains: Kykkos Monastery

TOP 25

A mural inside (left); mosaics covering an archway (middle) to the central courtyard (right)

THE BASICS

www.kykkos-museum.cy.net

🔲 E6

✉ West of Pedoulas, western Troodos

☎ 2294 2736

🕐 Jun–end Oct 10–6; Nov–end May 10–4

🍴 Cafés nearby

♿ Few

💰 Monastery free; museum moderate

❓ Gift shop with information

HIGHLIGHTS

● Famous icon, Eleousa, attributed to St. Luke
● Vivid gold mosaics on the cloister walls
● Archbishop Makarios III's tomb, above the monastery
● Commandaria and wine produced by the monks, available at the gift shop

Stunningly covered in vivid gold mosaic murals and sited high and alone in the thick pine forests of the Troodos Mountains of western Cyprus, splendid Kykkos is Cyprus' richest and most significant monastery.

Reasons to visit Kykkos Monastery's location is so spectacular that even at 1,318m (4,323ft) above sea level, it's still overlooked by higher ground. Cypriots make pilgrimages to Kykkos from all over Cyprus, as do Orthodox Christians from around the world, and it's well and truly on every tour-bus itinerary. Most come to see an icon attributed to Saint Luke and the monastery's two lovely courtyards with mosaic-covered walls. Today's monks enjoy modern comforts, yet even so the community has dwindled from hundreds to a handful. They spend their time making beautiful wines and ports that are sold in a gift shop in the lower courtyard.

The museum Built some 900 years ago to house the famous icon, Eleousa, the present monastery dates to the 19th century; fires destroyed earlier buildings. Within the monastery's museum, the icon has been encased in silver for over 200 years. It's thought that anyone attempting to gaze directly at it does so under sufferance of horrible punishment. The museum contains exhibitions on the monastery's history and extravagant religious regalia. Photography is not permitted within the museum but you're able to take photos of the vivid gold mosaics on the cloister walls.

More to See

Nicosia

AGIOS IOANNIS CATHEDRAL

Built in 1662, the inside of this splendid cathedral in the grounds of the Episcopal Precinct is decorated with vivid frescoes dating to the 18th century. Visitors are often lined up outside waiting to get in so arrive early.

✚ c3 ⊠ Plateia Archiepiskopou Kyprianou
🕐 Mon–Fri 8–12, 2–4, Sat 8–12 ✗ Cafés nearby ♿ Good 💷 Inexpensive

ARCHBISHOP MAKARIOS III CULTURAL CENTRE (BYZANTINE MUSEUM)

www.makariosfoundation.org.cy

The highlight of this museum is the expansive collection of exquisite icons gathered from across Cyprus. Dating from the 9th to the 19th centuries, it's the largest collection on the island. Also worth seeing is the collection of 6th-century Kanakaria Mosaics. The art gallery holds a good collection of paintings, lithographs and maps.

✚ c2 ⊠ Plateia Archiepiskopou Kyprianou
☎ 2243 0008 🕐 Mon–Fri 9–4.30, Sat 9–1 ✗ Cafés nearby ♿ Few 💷 Inexpensive

FAMAGUSTA GATE

Once the city's main southern and eastern entrance, this historic stone building was restored and reopened as a cultural centre and exhibition space. These days it's closed more often than it's open, however, if you're strolling by and it has its doors open, stick your head in for a look.

✚ c2 ⊠ Leoforos Athinon ✗ Café nearby
♿ Few 💷 Varies depending on event

HADJIGEORGAKIS KORNESIOS HOUSE (ETHNOGRAPHICAL MUSEUM)

This beautiful restored stone house once belonged to Hadjigeorgakis Kornesios, the Grand Dragoman of Cyprus, near the end of the 18th century. The dragoman's position was that of interlocutor between the ethnic communities and foreign powers, and the grandeur of the building reflects the power and respect he held.

✚ c3 ⊠ 20 Odos Patriarchou Grigoriou
☎ 2230 5316 🕐 Tue–Fri 8.30–3.30 (Thu to 5pm), Sat 9.30–3.30 ✗ Cafés nearby
♿ None 💷 Inexpensive

The Orthodox Agios Ioannis Cathedral

LAIKI GEITONIA

This small, renovated neighbourhood in the old city retains some character and charm despite the tacky souvenir stores. The tourist office is here, along with several good tavernas and bars.

➕ b3 ✉ Off Ledra Street and near Onasagoras, Nicosia old city ♿ Few

LEVENTIS MUNICIPAL MUSEUM

Another small but worthwhile museum, operated by the Nicosia Municipality, in an elegant stone neo-classical mansion dating to 1885. The Leventis has a fascinating exhibition on the city's 5,000-year history.

➕ b3 ✉ 17 Odos Ippokratous, Laiki Geitonia ☎ 2267 1997 🕐 Tue–Sun 10–4.40 🍴 Cafés and restaurants nearby ♿ Few 💰 Free

OMERIYE HAMAM

www.hamambaths.com

Constructed in the 16th century, this splendid stone *hamman* was used as a communal bath right up until 2002 when it was closed for renovation.

The baths were re-opened in 2003 and now resemble a spa more than a traditional *hammam*. A massage, steam and sauna are recommended, but at least take a look inside.

➕ b3 ✉ 8 Plateia Tillirias ☎ 2246 0570 or 2275 0550 🕐 Tue, Thu, Sat 9–9 (men); Wed, Fri, Sun 9–9 (women); Mon 11–7 (couples) 🍴 Restaurants and cafés nearby ♿ None 💰 Expensive

OMERIYE MOSQUE

This former medieval Agustinian Monastery of St. Marie was converted into Omeriye Mosque by the Ottoman Turks in the 16th century and still operates as Nicosia's main mosque. Visitors are welcome inside the beautiful stone building outside of prayer time; women should cover themselves and both genders should remove shoes. On Friday it's common for worshippers to be seen preparing and sharing communal lunches in the courtyard.

➕ b3 ✉ Plateia Tillirias 🕐 Anytime except prayer times 🍴 Restaurants and cafés nearby ♿ Few 💰 Free

The lively streets of Laiki Geitonia

Embroidered cloth at the Leventis Municipal Museum (below); Omeriye Mosque (opposite)

The High Troodos

AGIOS NIKOLAOU TIS STEGIS

The stunning 'St. Nicholas of the Roof' church takes its name from its unusual double roof. A large tiled roof protects the domed roof beneath it. Built in the 11th century, a cupola was added in the 12th century. Inside, vibrant frescoes date from the 11th to the 17th century.

✚ F6 ✉ 3.5km (2 miles) southwest of Kakopetria 🕒 Tue–Sat 9–4, Sun 11–4 🍴 Restaurants and cafés in Kakopetria ♿ Few ✋ Free

AGROS

At an altitude of 1,100m (3,608ft), this charming village is famous for its superb grapes, excellent fruit and vegetables, delicious sausages and cold cuts, traditional marmalades and sweets and, above all else, its roses. The village's rosewater, rose-scented perfume, soap and aromatic candles, and rose brandy and liqueur are celebrated here and abroad.

✚ G7 ✉ Southern Troodos Mountains 🍴 Restaurants and cafés ♿ None

CEDAR VALLEY AND PAFOS FOREST

Spectacularly situated in the western Troodos, this protected reserve is celebrated for its thick wooded forest that includes a vast valley of enormous old cedars. The road that snakes around the valley is excellent; its remote location means it still sees fairly few visitors passing through, which makes it possible to take it easy and stop the car and get out to appreciate the aromatic air and wonderful gradations in colour.

✚ E6 ✉ Western Troodos Mountains 🍴 Bring a picnic ♿ None

FIKARDOU

Declared a monument to protect its historic houses dating to between the 16th and 18th centuries, the delightful village of Fikdardou is a must-visit for architectural lovers. While several restored houses are open to visitors, it's a delight to simply wander around the place taking in the lovely details.

✚ H6 ✉ 35km (22 miles) southwest of Nicosia 🍴 Café in village ♿ None

Agros, standing at the head of a beautiful valley

Cedar Valley Forest, the last natural reserve of Cyprus cedar

KAKOPETRIA

This charming town in the lovely Solea Valley, on the lower slopes of the Troodos Mountains, has an atmospheric old quarter with narrow lanes and ramshackle houses that's a delight to explore. There's a creek that runs through town and local restaurants serve freshly caught trout.

➕ F6 ✉ Northern Troodos Mountains
🍴 Restaurants and cafés ♿ None

MACHAIRAS MONASTERY

It's a bit of a drive to get to Machairas but worth it for the spectacular setting alone. The views are actually better from the road above the monastery, with the bell tower dramatically sited below. Founded in the 12th century, the monastery's original buildings were destroyed by fires over the years. The current building only dates to the early 20th century, but nevertheless it is still splendid.

➕ H6 ✉ Near Fikardou, eastern Troodos mountains ⏰ Tue and Thu 9–12, Wed, Fri–Sun 8–5.30; Mon groups only 🍴 Cafés at Fikardou ♿ Few 👋 Free

MOUNT OLYMPOS

The highest mountain in Cyprus at 1,952m (6,402ft), Olympos is also the country's only peak to get sufficient snow for skiing and snowboarding. While a good fall can't be as relied upon as it once could, the snow is generally good enough for building snowmen, and after a snowfall the roads up to the Troodos are busy with visitors heading up for a look.

➕ F6 ✉ 55km (34 miles) from Limassol
🍴 Cafés at Troodos village ♿ None
👋 Ski lifts inexpensive

PANAGIA TOU ARAKA

While it takes a bit of an effort to drive here, albeit through some stunning scenery, the reward is a beautiful church boasting vivid frescoes, the most complete series of Byzantine-period wall paintings of any on the island, restored thanks to UNESCO. If the door is locked, call the caretaker who will let you in.

➕ G6 ✉ Lagoudera village ☎ 2265 2377 ⏰ Daily 10–4 🍴 Café in Lagoudera ♿ Few 👋 Free

The village of Kakopetria, dominated by a domed basilica

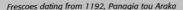
Frescoes dating from 1192, Panagia tou Araka

Nicosia's Old City

A stroll through the lovely, laidback streets of Nicosia's old city is the ideal introduction to this city's history, culture and politics.

DISTANCE: 3.5km (2 miles) **ALLOW:** 3 hours with stops

START

CYPRUS MUSEUM
✚ a3

END

LAIKI GEITONIA
✚ b3

❶ Begin your walk with an introduction to Cypriot history and a visit to the island's best and most important repository of archaeological finds, the excellent Cyprus Museum (▷ 68).

❽ Walk along Odos Ippokratous until you arrive at the end of the pedestrian area. Turn right and right again to explore the narrow lanes.

❷ From the museum, stroll along shady Leoforos Mouseiou to Pafos Gate, the entrance to the old city (▷ 69). Look up to your left and you may see Turkish Cypriot guards on 'the other side'.

❼ Continue along this street to Odos Ippokratous and Laiki Geitonia, a leafy neighbourhood of charming tavernas and shops. Stop at the Leventis Municipal Museum (▷ 74) to take in the city's history.

❸ Turn right at Pafos Gate, following the old wall along Leoforos Kostaki Pantelidi (note the car parks within the deep moats to your right) until you get to Plateia Eleftherias.

❻ From the checkpoint, turn right and right again. Follow this street with its appealing architecture up to Agia Faneromeni, where there's a café if you need refreshment.

❹ At the Square, turn left, crossing over to pedestrianized Ledra Street, old Nicosia's main shopping area.

❺ Follow this bustling street all the way down to the Green Line (the UN buffer zone between the north and south) and the Ledra Street (Odos Lidras) checkpoint.

78

Shopping

ANEMOESSA FINE FOOD PRODUCTS

www.anemoessa.com.cy
If it's made in Cyprus you'll be sure to find it here. Stocking beautifully-packaged, authentic Cypriot food and wine products, such as Zivania (grape liquor), Commandaria (▷ panel), and Glyka tou Koutaliou (homemade preserves), this is an ideal one-stop-shop for souvenirs.
➕ Off map ✉ 23 Odos Pindarou and K Stokkou, Nicosia ☎ 2287 7220

CHRYSALINIOTISSA CRAFTS CENTRE

Buy direct from Cypriot artists who practice their crafts, including glassmaking, ceramics, woodwork and jewellery design, in workshops where they apply modern techniques to traditional forms.
➕ Off map at c2 ✉ 2 Odos Demonakos, Nicosia

CYPRUS HANDICRAFT SERVICE

Make this government-operated handicrafts centre your first stop for traditional Cypriot handicrafts—you'll see everything here, from Lefkoniko woven textiles and Lefkara lace to beautiful ceramics and olive wood carvings. The quality is outstanding and you can be certain the products are original.
➕ c5 ✉ 186 Leoforos Athalassa, Nicosia
☎ 2230 5024

DEBENHAMS

Expect all the usual clothing lines, from Miss Sixty and Morgan for the girls to Emporio Armani and Diesel for the guys, along with accessories, perfume, cosmetics and homeware, plus a popular café.
➕ b4 ✉ 22 Leoforos Archiepiskopou Makariou III, Nicosia ☎ 2284 5000

DIACHRONIKI & NEA DIACHRONIKI

www.diachroniki.com
Inside three atmospheric old houses, these superb art galleries specialize in Cypriot art, old and new, traditional and contemporary, originals and prints.

COMMANDARIA

Cyprus is synonymous with Commandaria, a local sweet wine that can claim a history going back thousands of years, as well as garnering praise from Homer and Richard the Lionheart. This tawny wine gets its name from the Gran Commanderie, the region at the foothills of the Troodos Mountains where the grape varieties of *mavros* and *xynisteri* are grown. The grapes are sun-dried to increase their sugar and alcohol content and sometimes fortified to achieve the optimum alcohol content of around 14 per cent. KEO's Commandaria St. John is the most popular brand.

➕ b2 ✉ 84 Arsinois, 2B Odos Aristokyprou and 32 Odos Solonos, Nicosia ☎ 2268 0145, or 2266 5074

ESCLUSO

Head here for stylish hats, handbags and accessories from a range of designers, including the Cypriot owner's handmade designs.
➕ b4 ✉ 18 Leoforos Archiepiskopou Makariou III, Nicosia ☎ 2276 2202

IGIAS EDESMA

Preparing a picnic to take to the mountains or beach? Head here for fresh, locally grown organic fruit and vegetables, along with dried herbs, aloe vera, and eco-friendly cosmetics and essential oils.
➕ ♻ ✉ 1A Odos Romanou, near Hilton Hotel, Nicosia
☎ 2275 7538

KRAMA

Cypriot artist Skevi Afantiti creates strikingly innovative jewellery that is sold in exclusive boutiques around the world, including Athens' Benaki Museum. Buy yours from the source here.
➕ Off map ✉ 3A Odos Arnaldas, Nicosia
☎ 2276 1655

MARKS & SPENCER

Although slightly more expensive than the UK, if you find yourself having to pop into M&S for something at some point, you can rest assured it's

all here. It's exactly the same.

⊞ b4 ✉ 99 Leoforos Acropolis, Nicosia
☎ 2251 0900

MOUFFLON BOOKSHOP

www.moufflon.com.cy

The best bookshop in Cyprus is the place to head for compelling holiday reading or meaningful souvenirs. Moufflon has superb books on Cypriot archaeology, history, culture, society and politics, along with beautiful photographic books, cookbooks, travel books, fiction and more. You'll also find books by local authors, published by Moufflon, which are hard to get outside of Cyprus.

⊞ a3 ✉ 1 Odos Sofouli, Nicosia ☎ 2266 5155

NATAR & YASTROBNIK

www.nataryastrobnik.com

While famous for their beautiful fashions for men and women, the thing to buy from these impressive Cypriot designers, Demos Natar and Tomaz Yastrobnik, is their striking, handmade woollen dresses.

⊞ Off map ✉ Kyriakou Matsi, Nikis Centre, Nicosia
☎ 9915 6699

NICOS MICHALIAS CERAMIC AND TILE DESIGNS

www.michalias-studio.com

You'll find it hard to decide what to buy—all of the traditional hand-painted ceramics in here are exquisite, but the traditional Cypriot patterns are pretty special.

⊞ Off map ✉ 33 Lefkonos, Nicosia ☎ 2275 3900

NICOSIA MARKETS

Cypriot farmers descend on the old city several days a week to sell their fresh fruit and vegetables, homemade cheeses such as *halloumi*, smoked sausages like *loukanika*, along with fresh and dried herbs and spices. A great place to get picnic supplies, but it's also a wonderful place to take photos—you'll find few such lively and atmos-

pheric spots on the island.

⊞ b2 ✉ Plateia Ochi (Wed), Old Municipal Square (Sat), and Plateia Solomou (Sun), Nicosia ⊗ Best 9–1

NIKOS IOANNOU

www.ioannou-jewels.com.cy

If you've fallen in love with an ancient piece of jewellery at a Cyprus museum, the chances are you'll see something resembling it here. The island's best jewellery designer specializes in modern takes on classic Cypriot and Greek jewellery, and contemporary pieces crafted with a nod to classical styles.

⊞ b4 ✉ 79 Odos Onasagorou and 33 Leoforos Archiepiskopou Makariou III, Nicosia ☎ 2267 4023 or 2275 3251

PLAY

This is the most central store of this popular chain stocking Cypriot, Greek and international music CDs, DVDs, books, magazines, i-Pods and other music and digital accessories.

⊞ b3 ✉ Ledra Arcade, Ledra Street, Nicosia
☎ 2244 5696

VANILLA

This fabulous gift shop stocks gorgeous objects and materials for the home, from intricately decorated boxes to beautiful covered cushions. A great place for gifts.

⊞ Off map ✉ 40 Themistokli, Nicosia ☎ 2266 2660

Entertainment and Activities

ARTOS FOUNDATION

www.artosfoundation.org

This splendidly restored former bakery is now a vibrant arts and cultural centre that plays host to art and photography exhibitions, performances, film and video screenings, and fascinating seminars. This is the place to head if you're in any way artistically inclined and would like to engage with Cyprus' bohemian and intellectual set.

🞢 Off map ✉ 64 Odos Agios Omologites, Nicosia ☎ 2211 5455

BLING

www.blingcy.com

One of the capital's most popular dance clubs, Bling is a longstanding favourite that seems to remain cool despite changes in fashion and music trends. Different nights focus on different music, from hip-hop and R&B to Greek and international pop.

🞢 b2 ✉ 11 Odos Stasinou, Nicosia ☎ 9946 3368 🕓 Thu–Sat 11pm–late

CAVA NOSTRA

A popular wine bar where locals and expats alike go for a glass or two pre- or post-dinner. Try to get to one of their tasting nights when it's especially lively. You can also buy Cypriot wines here.

🞢 Off map a3 ✉ 5 Odos Sophouli, Nicosia ☎ 2237 4840 🕓 Mon–Wed 10–6, Thu–Sat 10–10

DA CAPO

This stylish minimalist café-bar is an old favourite. The casual atmosphere means you can pop in to refuel on the light dishes and snacks in between sight-seeing and shopping, check your email over a coffee, or head here for a drink in the evening. At night the lights go down a notch and the music is turned up; the locals dress up a bit, so it's wise to do the same.

🞢 b4 ✉ 30 Leoforos Archiepiskopou Makariou III, Nicosia ☎ 2275 7427 🕓 Daily 10–late

HERAKLIS GARDEN CAFÉ

Nicosia's famous ice cream stop is the place to take the kids before doing

MUSIC WITH SPIRIT

Greek folk music, known as *rembetika*, is as popular on the island as it is on the mainland. An organic style of music generally played on acoustic instruments such as the *bouzouki* and the guitar, the songs are generally about passion, loss, love and disappointment. The genre started in the 1920s when it was a rebellious form, but was widely accepted by the 1940s. A good night out listening to live *rembetika* sees spirited performances generally accompanied by spirits of the alcoholic kind.

the evening stroll along Ledra Street. There's also a playground in the garden in case you want to stay put and savour what many consider to be Cyprus' best ice cream.

🞢 b2 ✉ 110 Ledra Street, Nicosia ☎ 2266 4198 🕓 Daily 9–late

KALA KATHOUMENA

Locals like to sit outside at this simple café near Faneromeni Church. It's particularly popular with the old city's bohemian set and the old-timers from the area.

🞢 b2 ✉ Stou Papadopoulos, end of Ledra Street, Nicosia ☎ 2266 4654 🕓 Daily 9–late

MICROMANIA

www.micromania.com.cy

Hire a bike to cycle around the old city (a great way to explore its fascinating and mostly tranquil streets) or sign up for a cycling safari to the mountains or beaches.

🞢 b2 ✉ 15 Odos Stasinou, Nicosia ☎ 2266 1517

MONDO

A super-chic café-bar that attracts the city's style-conscious set, this is a fabulous place for a drink and a bit of people watching. Locals would lead you to believe it's the best of a bunch of places on the avenue.

🞢 b4 ✉ 37 Leoforos Archiepiskopou Makariou III, Nicosia ☎ 7777 8044 🕓 Daily 10–late

MOUSKIKI TAVERN FOR REMBETIKA

A must-do activity is a night out listening to traditional *rembetika* (Greek blues-style folk music) and Mouskiki Tavern is an institution. ➕ Off map ✉ Agiou Ilarionos, Nicosia ☎ 2234 9643 🕐 Fri and Sat night

NICOSIA RACE CLUB

www.nicosiaraceclub.com.cy Races take place twice a week in season at the Nicosia track. Call ahead to find out about special race days that can attract a rather swelling crowd. ➕ Off map ✉ Agios Dometios, Nicosia ☎ 2278 2727

PHAROS ARTS FOUNDATION MUSIC CONCERTS

www.pharosartsfoundation.org The busy Pharos Arts Foundation (✉ 24 Demosthenis Severis, Nicosia ☎ 2266 3871) organizes monthly concerts of classical music, featuring solo artists, quartets and even orchestras, which they sponsor and bring to the island. The programme features anything from chamber to choral music, and Nicosia's cultural set are normally in attendance. Concerts are held at various venues.

PLATO'S BAR

www.platosbar.com Plato's is a drinker's bar and the owner is a lover of beer, rock music and fast bikes. There's a great selection of brews including famous full-bodied Belgian brands. ➕ b2 ✉ 8–10 Odos Platanos, Nicosia ☎ 2266 6552 🕐 Daily 8pm–2am

SKIING MOUNT OLYMPOS

www.cyprusski.com Hire or bring your own ski gear on the slopes and, if you need one, book an excellent instructor—certified by the Cyprus Ski Federation—for some ski lessons on the gentle beginner's slopes. Snow has been unreliable in recent years and the seasons have been short, so if it's snowing while

you're on the island, do take a trip up to the Troodos Mountains so you can say you've swam and skied on the same day. Or at least have a snow fight. ➕ F6 ✉ Mount Olympos, Troodos Mountains

WALKING IN THE TROODOS

Midsummer is much too hot for this pastime, and as a result many visitors to Cyprus are enthusiatically turning to walking in the mountains in the cooler months. Consequently, there are now a few walking trails in the Troodos region designated by the Cyprus Tourism Organisation (▷ 12). Trails are not always that well marked on the ground; walkers therefore need to keep their wits about them and rely on their initiative at times. Large scale maps will be needed on most occasions. The British Ministry of Defence series is invaluable, available at the Department of Lands and Survey in Nicosia (☎ 2240 0600).

WEAVING MILL

Take your pick from a vibrant programme of live jazz, avant garde films and interesting lectures, or simply kick back with a glass of wine and thumb through a magazine. ➕ b2 ✉ 67–71 Odos Lefkonos, Nicosia ☎ 2276 2275

Restaurants

PRICES

Prices are approximate, based on a 3-course meal for one person.

€€€	over €60
€€	€20–60
€	under €20

AKAKIKO (€€)

The offering at this chic Japanese eatery also includes Korean, Chinese and even Malaysian dishes, but nobody seems to object to the fusion menu as the food is just so good.

🚇 b4 ✉ 9A Leoforos Archiepiskopou Makariou III, Nicosia ☎ 7777 8022
🕐 Mon–Fri lunch, dinner

CHOP'T (€)

This stylish little light-filled eatery, on the main pedestrian area in the old city, is an ideal lunch stop if you're worn out from exploring. The specialties here are big salads and if you don't find one you like you can devise your own.

🚇 b3 ✉ 207 Ledras Street, Nicosia ☎ 2281 8781
🕐 Daily lunch, dinner

COS'ALTRO (€€)

In the heart of the shopping strip, this chic café is perfect for resting those weary feet over coffee or assessing the damage to the credit card. While you are there, why not sample the excellent Italian pastas, delicious salads and

other café fare.
🚇 b4 ✉ 9 Leoforos Archiepiskopou Makariou III, Nicosia ☎ 7777 8055
🕐 Daily 7.30pm–11pm

ERODOS (€€)

www.visiterodos.com
This elegant stone building in the heart of the capital was once a quilt factory, but has now been transformed into a sophisticated place to hang out. The menu is lengthy including snacks, meze and full meals—everything from chicken wings to Greek salad—so there should be something to suit everyone here. There's also a wide range of Cypriot labels

THE LONG LUNCH

During weekends in Cyprus there is a tradition to have a family lunch. While visitors often baulk at the number of dishes on a local menu, when you have a group of more than eight, Cypriot food comes into its own—it's meant to be shared. Locals will order meze, a procession of dips and local specialties to share with bread. Dishes such as *saganaki* (*halloumi* cheese, served fried), *souvlaki* (meat and vegetables cooked on skewers), *kleftiko* (slow cooked lamb) as well as whatever fish is fresh will also play a part. Desserts such as *baklava* will follow—sometimes three hours later.

on the wine list.
🚇 b3 ✉ Patriarch Gregoriou 1, Nicosia ☎ 2275 2250
🕐 Tue–Sat 10am–2am, Sun 4pm–2am

IL FORNO (€)

Don't let the fast-food eatery vibe of the place deter you from trying the superb Italian at this casual restaurant on Ledra Street. The specialty of the house is pizza and the excellent pizzas are cooked in true Italian style, *al forno* (in the wood-fired pizza oven). There's also a short menu of tasty pastas if you're looking for something more filling.

🚇 b3 ✉ 216-18 Ledra Street, Nicosia ☎ 2245 6454
🕐 Daily lunch, dinner

KATHODON (€)

A decent Greek-Cypriot eatery near the Green Line; punters come more for the location and prime viewing spot than for the cuisine. It makes a perfectly fine lunch or dinner stop if your priority is atmosphere and people watching.

🚇 b2 ✉ 62D Ledra Street, Nicosia ☎ 2266 1656
🕐 Daily lunch, dinner

LATSI FISH TAVERN (€€)

Nicosia may not be on the sea, and this excellent taverna is nowhere near Latchi, but fresh seafood is guaranteed here; the owner prides himself on his fish bought daily at

the fish markets or right off the boat.

➕ Off map ✉ 1 Odos Agia Pavlou, Nicosia ☎ 2278 0937 🕐 Daily lunch, dinner

MATTHEOS (€€)

This down-to-earth eatery attracts a loyal crowd of locals who come for the hearty home-style lunches and lovely alfresco location near the diminutive mosque on this sunny square in the old city.

➕ b2 ✉ Plateia 28th October, Nicosia ☎ 2275 5846 🕐 Daily lunch only

MAZE (€–€€)

A sleek and stylish downtown eatery that is ideal for either a quick coffee, light snack or casual meal, and where the people watching is easily as good as the international cuisine on the menu.

➕ b4 ✉ 42 Odos Stasikratous, Nicosia ☎ 2244 7447 🕐 Daily lunch, dinner

MILL HOTEL RESTAURANT (€)

www.cymillhotel.com

The delightfully rustic room on the Mill Hotel's top floor is renowned for its whole trout served with lemon sauce, yet they also do excellent Cypriot and Greek standards along with succulent (and enormous) steaks and delicious pastas. While the hearty, large portions of home-cooked food is

fantastic, the atmospheric room with its big fireplace is reason enough to visit.

➕ F6 ✉ The Mill Hotel, 8 Milos, Kakopetria ☎ 2292 2536 🕐 Mon–Fri lunch only, Sat lunch, dinner

PLAKA (€€)

A seemingly never-ending meal of meze is the thing to try at this romantic restaurant, on a delightful square surrounded by traditional houses, in a suburb neighbourhood of Nicosia.

➕ Off map ✉ Makarios 6, Engomi ☎ 2235 2898 🕐 Mon–Sat dinner only

SITIO (€€)

Nicosia can't get enough of these chic casual café-bar-restaurants. And the tourists love them as much as the locals for their quality, good value cuisine and fascinating

people-watching opportunities, which are exceptional at this local favourite that attracts Nicosia's beautiful set.

➕ b3 ✉ 43 Leoforos Archiepiskopou Makariou III, Nicosia ☎ 2245 8610 🕐 Daily lunch, dinner

YIOLANDEL (€)

A simple local eatery, which attracts a loyal following for its hearty cuisine and no-nonsense, friendly atmosphere.

➕ F7 ✉ 3B Leoforos Makariou, Platres (near Pendeli Hotel) ☎ 2542 1720 🕐 Tue–Sun dinner only

ZANETTOS (€€)

www.zannetos.com

This traditional old city taverna is a must-have experience. Make a reservation well in advance (especially on weekends) and don't let the modest exterior put you off; once inside you'll find a big lively dining room packed with locals and the most delicious feast of meze on Cyprus. There is no written menu and a meal (feast!) is fixed price—the delicious dishes just keep coming and it seems like they'll never stop. Just let the staff know if there's anything you don't eat and sit back and enjoy.

➕ b2 ✉ 65 Odos Trikoupi, Nicosia old city ☎ 2276 5501 🕐 Tue–Sun dinner only

Tranquil Kyrenia (Keryneia/Girne), the walled city of Famagusta (Ammochostos/Gazimağusa) and the wild Karpaz Peninsula, are just a few of northern Cyprus' delights.

Northern Cyprus

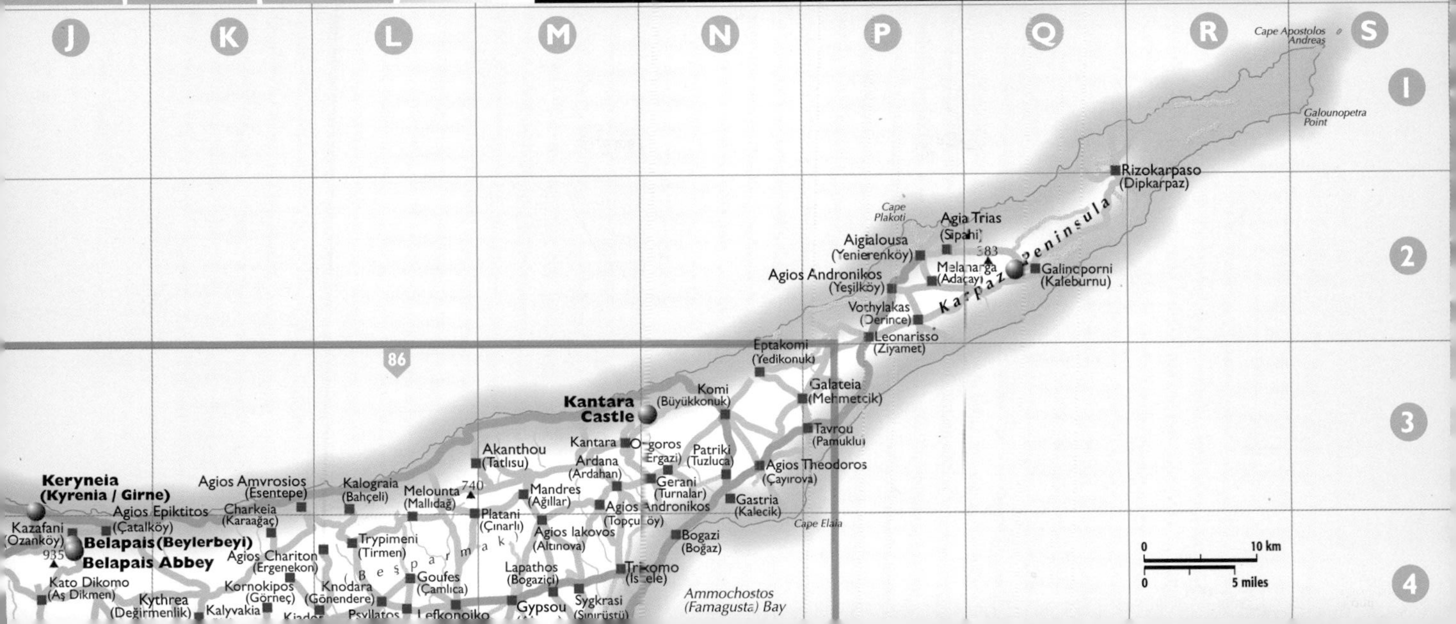

Kazafani (Ozanköy)
Kato Dikomo (Aş Dikmen)
Kythrea (Değirmenlik)

Keryneia (Kyrenia / Girne)
Agios Epiktetos (Çatalköy)
Belapais Abbey
Belapais (Beylerbey))

Agios Amvrosios (Esentepe)
Charkeia (Karaağaç)
Agios Chariton (Ergenekon)
Kornokipos (Görneç)
Knodara (Gönendere)
Psyllatos
Lefkoniko

Kalograia (Bahçeli)
Trypimeni (Tirmen)
Goufes (Çamlıca)
Lapathos (Boğaziçi)
Gypsou (Sınırüstü)
Sygkrasi (Sınırüstü)

Melounta (Mallidağ)
Akanthou (Tatlısu)
Platani (Çınarlı)
Agios Iakovos (Altınova)
Tricomo (İskele)

Mandres (Ağıllar)
Ardana (Ardahan)
Gerani (Turnalar)
Gastria (Kalecik)

Kantara Castle
Kantara (Büyükkonuk)
Komi (Büyükkonuk)
Ogoros Ergazi (Tuzluca)
Patriki (Tuzluca)
Agios Andronikos (Topçuköy)

Eptakomi (Yedikonuk)

Galateia (Mehmetçik)
Tavrou (Pamuklu)
Agios Theodoros (Çayırova)
Leonarisso (Ziyamet)
Vothylakas (Derince)

Agios Andronikos (Yenierenköy)
Aigialousa (Yeşilköy)

Agia Trias (Sipahi)
Malaina (Adaçay)
Galinoporni (Kaleburnu)

Rizokarpaso (Dipkarpaz)

Ammochostos (Famagusta) Bay

Cape Plakoti
Cape Elaia

Karpaz peninsula

383
240
86

Cape Apostolos Andreas
Galounopetra Point

0 10 km
0 5 miles

Belapais Abbey

TOP 25

The abbey ruins (left and opposite); chandeliers illuminate the nave (right)

THE BASICS

🕂 J4
✉ Belapais village centre
☎ 815 7540
🕐 Jun–end Sep 9–7; Oct–end May 9–4.30
🍴 Several restaurants and cafés nearby
♿ Few
💷 Moderate

HIGHLIGHTS

● The Refectory's rose window in the eastern wall
● Stone carvings, including a man being attacked by beasts, a woman reading and a monk wearing a cloak
● Pretty gardens filled with palm trees
● Spectacular views from the terrace

The ruins of Belapais Abbey are a breathtakingly beautiful Gothic masterpiece. Equally impressive is its stunning location on the Pentadaktylos Mountains' northern slopes with spectacular views of the coast below.

The ruins Augustinian monks fleeing Jerusalem founded the splendid abbey at the end of the 12th century and its importance lasted for some 300 years. Substantial parts collapsed long ago and the lovely cloister of 18 pointed arches is partly ruined. Yet it is still a magnificent sight, especially when illuminated at night.

Sights On the north side of the Abbey is the monk's refectory, where the vaults of the roof appear to spring lightly from their capitals. Tall elegant windows look out to the northern shore, and an exquisite pulpit reached by an intricate stairwell is ingeniously built into the wall. On the northern side of the courtyard the church, dating to the 13th century, is the best-preserved and has 15th-century murals. On the other side fascinating carvings include a monkey and cat under a pear tree.

Literary connections The village itself is famous for its former resident, British travel writer Lawrence Durrell, who lived here from 1953–56. In 1995 forest fires swept throughout the mountains, swiftly advancing on Belapais (▷ 100), living up to the description in his celebrated book *The Bitter Lemons of Cyprus*, in which he wrote 'two things spread quickly: gossip and a forest fire'.

Famagusta

HIGHLIGHTS

● Striking fortifications and gates, including the Sea Gate, Canbulat Gate and Land Gate
● Elegant Lala Mustafa Paşa Mosque
● Carved winged lion of St. Mark hanging over the Citadel's entrance

TIP

● When exploring the fortifications watch out for the unguarded parapets, take water, and explore during the cooler parts of the day.

The walled city of Famagusta (Ammochostos/ Gazimağusa) is a supreme example of surviving medieval military architecture. Gothic church mosques, church ruins and sandstone buildings add to its fascination.

History To enter Famagusta's massive walls is to pass through history, through the times of the Lusignans, Genoese, Venetians and the long Ottoman siege in 1570–71. While it's believed the city was first established between 285–300BC by King Ptolemy Philadelphus II, not far from Salamis, it's thought the present city was built on the ancient ruins of Arsenoe, following the sacking of Salamis by Arab raiders in 648AD.

What to see Apart from the fashion boutiques and cafés lining the main street, the central square

Clockwise from far left: crumbling ruins of Gothic-style churches are a symbol of Famagusta's old city; Famagusta's 16th-century Venetian walls; sunshades shield you from the hot sun, Famagusta beach; Othello's Tower, the oldest building in Famagusta

and surrounding cobblestone streets appear to have changed little over time. Palm trees shade crumbling medieval church domes and elegant spires that have been transformed into minarets. The massive Lala Mustafa Paşa Mosque is the most impressive, along with ruins of former churches turned into mosques by the Ottomans. Most engaging are the fortifications themselves. Created by the Lusignans, these were altered by the Venetians when they took over in 1489 and completely renovated the boundary walls. Experts in military architecture, they lowered the ramparts, increased their thickness, and removed all features vulnerable to cannon fire.

Citadel While it's a joy simply to wander the city's streets, don't miss the citadel, known as Othello's tower, from Shakespeare's play partly set in Cyprus.

THE BASICS

✚ N5
🍴 Restaurants and cafés in the old city and new town
♿ Few
✋ Expensive
❓ Explanatory signs at most sites

Famagusta: Lala Mustafa Paşa Mosque

The intricate façade (left) with a stunning central window (middle); Gothic hall (right)

THE BASICS

✚ N5
✉ Naim Efendi Sokagi
🕐 Daily, except during prayer times
🍴 Restaurants and cafés on the square
♿ Good
🎫 Free

HIGHLIGHTS

● Splendid Gothic façade with its striking arches and intricately detailed decoration
● The stunning central six-light window of the western front
● The enormous interior featuring a fine Gothic nave

This somewhat awe-inspiring sandstone structure may have been a mosque for over 400 years, yet the Lala Mustafa Paşa Mosque is still very much a glorious example of Gothic architecture.

Origins Named after Lala Mustafa, the victorious commander of the Ottoman Turks when they finally broke into Famagusta in 1571, this splendid Lusignan cathedral on Famagusta's central plaza, Namik Kemal Square, is the city's star attraction.

Highlights The single minaret may be well executed but it is out of place atop the damaged left-side spire. Even so, it is still possible to admire this elegant example of ecclesiastical architecture and one of the finest churches in the east. Highlights include a brilliant central six-light window and three beautiful front portals with exquisite intricate detail. The portals lead to the impressive interior, where Muslim simplicity has enabled the fine Gothic nave to survive but led to the loss of the extravagant Christian decoration. The clear glass arched windows are still decorated with pretty shaped patterns that are more like the Arabesque mashrabiyya (latticework) rather than the traditional stained glass associated with Gothic cathedrals.

Show respect You may visit the interior outside of prayer times but dress modestly (women should cover their heads, arms and legs and men should wear trousers and shirt sleeves) and remove your shoes out of respect. If you have come unprepared, you can borrow a cloak at the entrance.

The remains of Kantara Castle loom high above the Karpaz Peninsula

Kantara Castle

With breathtaking views of the coastline, the wild Karpaz Peninsula, and the villages and coast of the southeast, Kantara Castle has one of the most dramatic settings of all of Cyprus' castles.

Stunning location Standing tall some 600m (1,968ft) above sea level at the eastern end of the Besparmak Mountains, Kantara's dramatic location would be sufficient reason to visit, if it weren't so much fun to explore the castle ruins themselves.

Medieval fortress Built around 1191 as a lookout to protect against Arab raiders, Kantara (meaning 'arch' or 'bridge' in Arabic) is the most easterly of northern Cyprus' great Lusignan fortresses, of which there are three in total, including Buffavento and St. Hilarion castles. It was Kantara's location with such far-reaching views that gave the Lusignan garrison control of the Karpaz Peninsula.

What to see While much of the castle is in ruin, the formidable outer wall is fairly intact. After entering through a ruined barbican and two imposing towers, steps lead in to vaulted chambers and medieval toilets. Make sure you climb to the highest point to see the remains of a Gothic window.

Mystic atmosphere The castle's crumbling grey stone ramparts crown dramatic limestone crags, making for an atmospheric and rather eerie site. If it's windy, which it often is (wear shoes with a good grip and hold on tight), the wild weather only adds to the drama of the site.

THE BASICS

✚ N3
✉ Northeast Cyprus, near Kantara village
🕐 May–Oct daily 10–5; Nov–Apr 9–2.45
🍴 Café in Kantara village
♿ None
✋ Moderate

HIGHLIGHTS

● Breathtaking vistas of the surrounding coast and villages
● The formidable and fairly intact castle walls
● The remains of a Gothic window
● The vaulted chambers, including medieval toilets

Kyrenia: Harbour and Castle

TOP
25

**With its delightful quayside, lined with
stone buildings with wooden balconies
and shuttered windows opening on to the
sea, Kyrenia (Keryneia/Girne) has one of
the most bewitching harbours in the Med.**

A certain charm For many, Kyrenia is a highlight
of a trip to northern Cyprus. While the harbourfront
exudes atmosphere and the tiny charming backstreets are worth a wander, imposing Kyrenia
Castle is the key sight.

Kyrenia Castle Independent until conquered by
Salamis in 312BC, Kyrenia became a Christian city
during Roman times, and a small Byzantine church
stands within Kyrenia Castle. While excavations
date to the 7th century BC, most of the present
castle was built by the Lusignans from 1192,

Clockwise from far left: the perfect picture, Kyrenia Harbour; a coat-of-arms carved on the fortified walls of Kyrenia Castle; narrow passageways concealed behind the walls of the castle; the view from the castle over the harbour; pretty restaurants line the quayside

although the Venetians are given credit for its formidable structure and impregnable walls. After entering via the gatehouse, your first instinct will be to explore the ramparts and take in the marvellous views across town and to sea. Within the castle, visit the dungeons and displays. The earliest signs of Kyrenia's settlement stretch back to Neolithic times although it was during the Bronze Age Anatolian civilizations that it grew. In the east wing are finds from a Bronze Age tomb at Kirni, and a lifesize representation of the Neolithic village at Vrysi. The Shipwreck Museum is the highlight, with its ancient ship dating to 300BC and fascinating objects found on board.

Time to relax After exploring the sights, linger over a long seafood lunch in the sun at a quayside restaurant, with the boats bobbing nearby.

THE BASICS

🔢 J3
🍴 Restaurants and cafés on the harbour
♿ Few
🕐 Castle daily May–Oct 9–7; Nov–Apr 9–1, 2–4.45
💰 Castle moderate
🛈 Girni Harbour, tel 815 2145

Karpaz Peninsula

Byzantine churches, some with beautiful interiors, are a feature of the isolated landscape

THE BASICS

- N3–S1
- Most northeastern part of Cyprus
- Cafés in Dipkarpaz village and overlooking some beaches
- Few

HIGHLIGHTS

- Sandstone Byzantine churches overlooking the sea
- Creamy sand beaches and pretty fishing coves
- Apostolos Andreas Monastery at the end of the road on Cape Zafer, sacred to both Turkish-Cypriots and Greek-Cypriots

With its wild rocky coastline boasting pretty aquamarine coves, Byzantine churches, crumbling stone houses, sandy windswept beaches and lush countryside, this easternmost part of Cyprus is its most remote and most beautiful.

The panhandle This isolated peninsula known as 'the panhandle', some 80km (49 miles) long, is Cyprus' most pristine area. Its inaccessibility—there's just one major road passing through—has helped preserve its natural beauty. The beaches are another highlight, from tiny crescents of sand skirting small rocky fishing coves to a long stretch of creamy sand, backed by dunes, best enjoyed from picturesque Galounopetra point.

Byzantine churches The far-flung cape is home to a number of beautiful sandstone Byzantine churches, all easily visited. Some are well pre-served with structures intact and tiled roofs, while others are in ruins, their walls crumbling around them and vivid mosaic floors exposed to the elements. The best include 5th-century Agios Filon Church, the sole survivor of the ancient Phoenician city Karpasia; 5th-century Agios Trias Basilica near Sipahi village with stunning patterned mosaic floors (note the tiles featuring 'flip-flop' like Roman sandals); Kanakaria Church near Boltashli village, also famous for its mosaics, although locals claim the best have been stolen; chalky white 15th-century Agios Thrysos Church, empty except for a few wooden pews; and nearby a smaller ruined medieval chapel enjoys spectacular sea views.

TOP 25

The mosque conceals lavish Christian architecture and the decoration permitted by Islam

Northern Nicosia: Selimiye Mosque

This magnificent mosque, once the Cathedral of Santa Sophia, and one of the finest examples of French church architecture, is yet another example of the Lusignans' impressive legacy in northern Nicosia.

Background Once a Christian masterpiece before the Ottoman Turks transformed it into a mosque, this stunning building was once considered the finest cathedral of its kind in the Near East. Construction of the original cathedral began in 1208 but wasn't completed until 117 years later, and even then it wasn't entirely finished. In actuality it was never quite completed, with work still being carried out long after its consecration. While the overall enormity of the structure is astonishing, it's the intricate and elaborate detail, especially of the portal, that will impress.

Minarets However breathtakingly beautiful the building is, what appears odd is the discordant elevation of the splendid windows, portals and buttresses, the reason being the soaring minarets; notable landmarks in the old walled city—you can even see the minarets from southern Nicosia. Their imposition on the west front by the Ottoman Turks reflects the momentous events of 1570–71 when the Ottomans subjugated the city.

Changes Everything changed with the arrival of the Ottoman Turks. All the extravagant Christian decoration of the cathedral's interior was destroyed and soon after work began on the minarets.

THE BASICS

✚ b2

✉ Selimiye Sokagi (the centre of the old city), Nicosia

🕙 Daily except during prayer times

🍴 Café on the square and in the Han nearby

♿ Few

💰 Free

HIGHLIGHTS

● The magnificent church structure, which is a masterpiece in Lusignan cathedral architecture
● The splendid detail of the exterior with its intricate decorations, especially around the portal, and the striking flying buttresses

St. Hilarion Castle

TOP
25

Crumbling St. Hilarion Castle, draped over four levels of the slopes of Mount Didymos

THE BASICS

✚ J4

✉ West of Kyrenia on the road to Nicosia

🕐 May–end Sep daily 9–6; Oct–end Apr 9–4.30; last admission one hour before

🍴 Café on site although not always open

♿ None

💷 Moderate

❓ Brochure at ticket office

HIGHLIGHTS

● Breathtaking views of the coast and mountains
● The atmospheric and almost eerie aura around these crumbling ruins
● St. John's Tower and the Queen's Window; this is your reward for a climb that's particularly challenging in the summer heat

Perched precariously on one of the highest points of the northern coast, these beguiling castle ruins aren't easily visited, yet your efforts will be rewarded with truly spectacular coastal vistas.

Turbulent history Named after St. Hilarion, a recluse who found refuge here, a monastery was first established on the hill in the 11th century. Built to protect the island from Arab attacks that occurred between the 7th and 11th centuries, the castle was besieged and taken by Richard the Lionheart in 1191 when its Byzantine ruler Isaac Comnenos surrendered. Today, the Turkish Cypriot military controls the heights around the castle.

Exploring the site Later fortified and extended by the Lusignans, the lower ward housed their garrison and horses. A tunnel leads from here to the middle ward and a small Byzantine church. Steps descend to a hall that may have been a refectory or banqueting chamber, now used for exhibitions, while adjacent is a belvedere and café with stupendous views. St. John's Tower, in a particularly precipitous location, can be reached by a series of rocky stairs while the Queen's Window is a welcoming place to rest and take in the scenery.

Views The climb up steep rocky stairs between the lower, middle and upper wards is compensated with magnificent views. Cyprus' northern shore is directly below, mainland Turkey is visible in the clear light of the cooler months, and to the east and west are a spectacular line of peaks.

Ruins of the ancient city (left); detail of a mosaic found in the basilica (right)

Salamis

Dating to the 7th century BC, Salamis was the first city of Cyprus, and the superb Roman theatre, marble colonnades, beautiful bathhouse and vivid mosaics are a mere hint of its grandeur.

The first city Archaeologists may argue over whether Salamis was established in the 11th or 7th century BC, however, legend has it that the founder of ancient Salamis was Greek hero Teucer, brother of Ajax and son of Telamon. What's indisputable is that the important trading centre was the island's first city until Roman occupation centuries later when Pafos was made capital, only to have its status restored in AD350 by the Byzantines who named it Constantia.

Former greatness Continual rebuilding after earthquakes and attacks by Arab raiders left the city in ruins, but some impressive sights remain. The Roman theatre boasts tiers of seats rising to a striking height, while a bathhouse has impressive vents and hypocausts opening on to a gymnasium complex, whose rows of marble columns make it one of the most atmospheric. Damaged by earthquakes, it was remodelled in Byzantine times, only to collapse later; the columns seen today were re-erected in the 1950s. South of the theatre, the immense granite columns of the forum lie across the site. The agora is near the voutra, a 7th-century cistern, and close by is the Temple of Zeus. Northeast toward the sea is an early Christian basilica. Across the road is the Royal Necropolis with several tombs.

THE BASICS

✚ M5

✉ 10km (6 miles) north of Famagusta

🕐 May–Oct daily 9–6; Nov–Apr 9–1, 2–4.45

🍽 Restaurants and cafés on the road into Famagusta

♿ Few

💰 Expensive

❓ Brochure at ticket office

HIGHLIGHTS

● An impressive Roman theatre with intact tiered seating
● The baths and gymnasium complex with its colonnades of marble columns, remains of swimming pools, hot and cold rooms and latrines
● Striking marble statues and mosaics

More to See

BELAPAIS

The home of Belapais Abbey, beguiling Belapais (Beylerbeyi) was also the home of celebrated British author and travel writer, Laurence Durrell from 1953 to 1956. It was here in this charming village of old stone houses and narrow winding lanes that he wrote *The Bitter Lemons of Cyprus*, about life in the village. The café he famously wrote about still stands on the square opposite the abbey.

✚ J4 ✉ In the mountains above Kyrenia
🍴 Restaurants and cafés ♿ Few ❓ Abbey ticket office has useful information

MORFOU

Set in one of the country's most agriculturally fertile areas, famous for its red soil and fragrant orange blossoms, citrus fruits and strawberries, laidback Morfou (Güzelyurt) is best known for its Byzantine-era Monastery of St. Mamas and Icon Museum, and its Museum of Nature and Archaeology with displays of finds from the ruins of Soloi and Palace of Vouni.

✚ G4 🍴 Cafés ♿ Few

NORTHERN NICOSIA: BÜYÜK HAMAM

Blink and you'll miss this 14th-century stone bathhouse set well below street level. Once the Church of St. George, the atmospheric old building displays typical Turkish domes and a rather retro sign out front. Men can get a scrub and use the sauna and steam rooms daily, but women's day is limited to Friday only. Hours are displayed outside.

✚ b2 ✉ Mousa Orfenbey Sokagi 🕐 Jun–end Sep 7.30–1, 4–6; Oct–end May 8–1, 2–6
🍴 Cafés nearby at Büyük Han ♿ None
✋ Moderate for scrub/sauna; free to look

NORTHERN NICOSIA: BÜYÜK HAN

A former inn for travellers and traders, this exquisitely restored stone building was commissioned in 1572 by Lala Mustafa Paşa, Cyprus' first Ottoman governor. Craft shops, boutiques and cafés now occupy the old stables and former accommodation.

✚ b2 ✉ Arasta Sokagi 🕐 Sat–Thu 8–8, Fri 8–midnight 🍴 Café-bars in courtyard
♿ Few (ground level only) ✋ Free

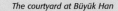

Peace and tranquility in the courtyard of Belapais Abbey

The courtyard at Büyük Han

NORTHERN NICOSIA: LAPIDARY MUSEUM

The Venetian-influenced architecture, including Moorish-style arched windows and decorative stone carvings, suggests that this grand, two-storey, stone building was once home to a wealthy Venetian family and may also have been a guesthouse for pilgrims and travellers.

🔼 b2 ✉ Northeast of the Selimiye Mosque ☎ 228 9629 ⏰ Jun–end Sep 9–12, 3.30–5.45; Oct–end May 9–12.30, 1.30–4.45 🍴 Cafés nearby on main square 🦽 Few 💵 Inexpensive

NORTHERN NICOSIA: MEVLEVI TEKKE (ETHNOLOGICAL MUSEUM)

This modest stone building was the home of the 13th-century Islamic sect, the Whirling Dervishes, who spin themselves into a trance. Turkish president Kemal Atatürk banned the group in 1925, however, in recent years the dance has been increasingly celebrated in Turkey. On display here are beautiful musical instruments and traditional costumes.

🔼 b1 ✉ 100m (110 yards) south of Kyrenia Gate ☎ 228 9629 ⏰ Jun–end Sep Mon–Fri 9–2; Oct–end May 9–1, 2–4.45 🍴 Cafés nearby 🦽 Few 💵 Inexpensive

SOLOI

After surviving Persian attacks, the 11th-century city of Soloi (Soli) was destroyed by Arab raiders during the 7th century. Excavations have unearthed a palace, theatre, temples, agora, church and necropolis.

🔼 F5 ✉ (16km) 10 miles southwest of Morfou ☎ 727 8035 ⏰ May–Sep daily 9–6; Oct–Apr 9–1, 2–4.45 🦽 None 💵 Moderate

VOUNI PALACE

Almost as spectacular as the views is the edge-of-your-seat drive to this important archaeological site. Built by a pro-Persian Phoenician king, the 137-room palace boasted enormous apartments, a bathhouse, storerooms and garrison; these days little remains.

🔼 E5 ✉ Near Soloi ⏰ May–Sep daily 9–5; Oct–Apr 9–1, 2–4.45 🦽 None 💵 Moderate

Mevlevi Tekke, built in the early 17th century as a monastery

Traditional costume displayed in the Mevlevi Tekke Museum

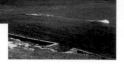

Kyrenia to Karpaz Peninsula and Cape Zafer

Travel along mountain ridges, past countryside blanketed with wild-flowers, rocky aquamarine coves and windswept sandy beaches.

DISTANCE: 190km (118 miles) **ALLOW:** all day with stops

START

KYRENIA
✚ J3

❶ From Kyrenia (▷ 94) drive east on the coast toward Çatalköy, stopping at Six Mile Beach, Eight Mile Beach and Twelve Mile Beach, named by the British during the colonial period when they established posts to mark distances from Kyrenia.

❷ Head to Tatlisu village, now surrounded by villa developments, from where it's a 19km (12-mile) drive to Kaplica. Here the road climbs steeply to Kantara village.

❸ A 6km (3.5-mile) edge-of-your-seat drive takes you from Kantara village along the mountain ridge to Kantara Castle (▷ 93) on a bumpy track.

❹ From Kantara village, take the dirt road south down the mountain, a valley of olive groves, wild herbs and grazing sheep before you, to Büyükkonuk village.

END

CAPE ZAFER
✚ S1

❽ Follow the coastal road along the windswept coast, calling into Apostolos Andreas Monastery on the way to Cape Zafer, the remote easternmost point of Cyprus.

❼ Follow the road northeast via Dipkarpaz, detouring to 5th-century Agios Philon, then through breath-taking country to Capa Kasa to the island's most beautiful beach, a stretch of cream sand backed by dunes.

❻ Head to Yenierenköy to enjoy the aquamarine coves and the exquisite ruined churches of Agios Thyrsos and Agios Trias.

❺ Drive northeast via Mehmetçik to the beautiful Karpaz Peninsula (▷ 96), stopping at Boltashli village for the splendid Byzantine church of Kanakaria.

NORTHERN CYPRUS   DRIVE

Shopping

BANDABULYA

The covered bazaar, or Bandabulya, was the old city's main marketplace for decades. Many locals still come here to buy their fruit and vegetables, however, it's also a great place to pick up some Turkish Delight, dates, nuts and preserves, and traditional souvenirs of your trip, such as olive soap and other *hammam* products.
➕ b2 ✉ Old Centre, Nicosia

BAYRAMOGLU

These Turkish-made shoes (for men and women), handbags and accessories can range from the stylish to the silly, and might not be to everyone's taste, but they're very reasonably priced.
➕ a1 ✉ 41 Osman Pasa Caddesi, Nicosia ☎ 227 3835

BÜYÜK HAN

This splendid restored stone building in a former *caravanserail* (merchant's inn) is now one of the most charming places to shop in the old city for northern Cypriot handicrafts, such as colourful handwoven baskets, vibrant striped textiles, jewellery and other souvenirs. Look out for the traditional puppeteer upstairs. There are a few cafés to rest your weary feet and just outside the main entrance there are several shops selling spices, dried fruits and nuts and local jams.
➕ b2 ✉ Arasta Sokagi, Nicosia

CYPRUS CORNER

Full of character, this delightful shop is jam-packed with fascinating antiques, bric-a-brac and jewellery—all with a story behind them—from well-used wooden bread-making bowls to lovely goats bells.
➕ b2 ✉ Old Centre, Nicosia ☎ 227 9347

FANUS

You'll feel like you've entered a Middle Eastern bazaar in this beautiful shop that sells gorgeous ceramics and handicrafts. There are other souvenirs that are more Turkish than Cypriot, such as beautifully decorated tiles, bowls and plates with Ottoman-era patterns, and lovely Oriental lamps.
➕ J3 ✉ 32 Canbulat Sokak, Kyrenia ☎ 815 0365

GORDES

Cyprus' best carpet shop stocks a fantastic range of beautiful Oriental carpets and Turkish kilims that you won't see anywhere else in Cyprus.
➕ J3 ✉ 32 Canbulat Sokak, Kyrenia ☎ 815 8413

NAKKAS

Do you like exploring your grandparents' garage or loft? Well this charmingly cluttered shop is crammed to the brim with antiques and bric-a-brac, from engraved copper coffee pots to intricately decorated brass trays. It's a delight to rummage around in.
➕ J3 ✉ 32 Canbulat Sokak, Kyrenia ☎ 815 9163

RESAT

www.resataltinor.com
Resat are gold and diamond jewellery specialists that stock some exquisite pieces. Many of the elaborate items you won't see in the south as they lean more toward the Oriental and Turkish styles. The stunning necklaces are particularly eye-catching.
➕ J3 ✉ Ziya Rizki Caddesi, Kyrenia ☎ 815 4155

TASTY SOUVENIRS

A tasty take-home is a box of Turkish Delight, or *lokum*, the signature sweet of Turkey. Made from starch and sugar, the soft, jelly-like consistency sees it always coated with icing sugar to keep the pieces from sticking. Popular flavours include rosewater and lemon, as well nutty flavours such as pistachio. You can, of course, buy it in the south too, where it's known as *loukoumi* or 'Cyprus Delight', neither names being a popular conversation topic among the Turkish population.

Entertainment and Activities

AMPHORA SCUBA DIVING

www.amphoradiving.com
Located at Escape Beach, 8km (5 miles) west of Kyrenia, Amphora offer wreck diving to the Zenobia wreck and PADI dive courses, in addition to other exciting activities such as jeep safaris and paragliding.

🔼 H3 ✉ Escape Beach, Karaoglanoglu ☎ 864 7569

BIG TOW WATERSPORTS

This popular family-owned watersports company offers a wide range of watery activities, including wakeboarding, waterskiing and knee-boarding.

🔼 H3 ✉ Green Coast Holiday Village, Alsancak ☎ 845 3713

DELCRAFT

www.ecotourismcyprus.com
In addition to the rustic accommodation in a big old traditional stone house, Delcraft offers northern Cyprus' first eco-village experience, where you can share in the traditional lifestyle of rural Cypriots. Have lots of fun, while taking part in the fascinating activities on offer—walks with local shepherds behind their flocks of sheep, donkey treks, olive-picking, and breadmaking with the village baker.

🔼 N3 ✉ Büyükkonuk village, Karpaz Peninsula ☎ 383 2038

HIGHLINE PARAGLIDING

www.highlineparagliding.com
A family-owned company, these highly experienced, licensed professional pilots have been running paragliding tours (solo and tandem) for nine years. Their clients range from children to even 100-year old ladies.

🔼 J3 ✉ Kyrenia Harbour ☎ 855 5672

KORINEUM GOLF AND COUNTRY CLUB

www.korineumgolf.com
Created within a beautiful natural forest with views of the Mediterranean Sea, this is northern Cyprus' best golf course, the first 18-hole course to be built in the north. In addition to the lovely lush grounds, there's a golfing

BIRD IS THE WORD

Northern Cyprus is one of the best bird-watching spots in the eastern Mediterranean, boasting over 40 native species. Its position in the Mediterranean sees it on the path of several migration flyways hosting an additional 200 species and millions of birds every year. The Karpaz Peninsula in particular is a fine area to see such species as shrikes, wheatears, chats and, more commonly, barred warblers, thrush nightingales and citrine wagtails—all in beautiful, rugged surroundings.

academy, pro shop and club house.

🔼 J3 ✉ Esentepe, near Kyrenia ☎ 600 1500

KYRENIA'S CAFÉS

There are a dozen or so café-bars lining the water-front of Kyrenia's beautiful harbour, which make a wonderful place to while away a few hours with a Turkish coffee or cold beer in hand while you watch the boats bobbing on the water.

🔼 J3 ✉ Kyrenia Harbour

NORTHERN CYPRUS HERBARIUM

This botanist's research centre displays over 1,200 native species of plants including wildflowers found in northern Cyprus that have never before been seen in other parts of the world.

🔼 J4 ✉ Alevkaya Forest Station, Kyrenia mountain range ☎ No phone

ORNEK TOURS

www.ornekholidays.eu
This trusted and long-established specialist travel agency runs bird-watching and botany walking tours (among others) that are particularly popular with Europeans. They also offer historical and cultural themed tours with knowledgeable guides.

🔼 J3 ✉ Ufuk Apt 2, Mete Adanir Caddesi, Kyrenia ☎ 815 8969

Restaurants

PRICES

Prices are approximate, based on a 3-course meal for one person.

€€€ over YTL115
€€ YTL28–115
€ under YTL138

THE ADDRESS (€€)

Reserve a table on the terrace at this stunning seaside restaurant and then sit back and enjoy the authentic Turkish-Cypriot dishes, which include juicy kebabs and fresh seafood.

✚ J3 ✉ 13 Ali Aktas Sokak, Karaoglanoglu, near Kyrenia ☎ 822 3537 ⏰ Daily lunch, dinner

AZAFRAN (€)

A longstanding favourite with northern Cyprus' British expatriates, this delightful café pulls in the crowds for its ploughman's lunches, scones, welcoming fireplace, foreign newspapers and internet access.

✚ J4 ✉ Zafer Sokak, Belapais ☎ 815 7679 ⏰ Daily

BELLAPAIS GARDENS RESTAURANT (€€)

www.bellapaisgardens.com
This is northern Cyprus' best restaurant; dine here and you'll see why. There's a long menu of delicious local specialties and international dishes, an excellent wine list that includes local wines, a charmingly decorated room with a fireplace for winter months, and warm, welcoming and informed service. Come for lunch and you'll get to enjoy the spectacular views down to the coast.

✚ J4 ✉ Crusader Road, Belapais ☎ 815 6066 ⏰ Daily lunch, dinner

CAFÉ DÜKKAN (€)

The warm service, laid-back atmosphere and menu of European café standards (salads, pastas and sandwiches) and Turkish dishes make this casual arty café popular with both locals and the British expat community. When you pay your bill, pick up a few of the brochures by the cash register advertising local art exhibitions and other interesting activities that it's difficult to hear

'PEACH KEBAB'

One of the most unusual dishes you will see on a northern Cyprus menu is the uniquely Cypriot 'peach kebab'. But no, it's not some odd grilled fruit dish, it's actually the result of a misunderstanding about the name of the dish. It was a 'Chef Ali's' specialty and 'Chef Ali' became 'eftali'–'peach' in Turkish. Made from patties of ground lamb, red and green peppers as well as spices, the special ingredient is sheep's stomach lining, which may make some feel peach might have been a better choice.

about otherwise.

✚ J3 ✉ Mete Adanir Caddesi, Kyrenia ☎ 815 2200 ⏰ Daily lunch, dinner

CENAP (€€)

The staff's dancing may not be as spontaneous as advertised but the live music, convivial atmosphere, traditional Cypriot cuisine and a very filling 'full kebab' all combine to make a meal here a satisfying experience in more ways than one.

✚ J3 ✉ 27 Ankara Caddesi, Kyrenia ☎ 821 8417 ⏰ Daily lunch, dinner

CYPRUS HOUSE (€€)

At the east coast's finest restaurant, you can expect superb Turkish-Cypriot dishes, which are served up in a traditionally decorated restaurant designed to look like an inviting old farmhouse.

✚ N5 ✉ Opposite the courthouse, Famagusta ☎ 366 4845 ⏰ Daily dinner only

DB (€)

The food won't win any awards but the Turkish-Cypriot and international dishes are hearty and generous in size. What this eatery really has going for it is its excellent location, with stunning views (especially at night) of the Lala Mustafa Paşa Mosque.

✚ N5 ✉ Naim Efendi Sokagi, Famagusta ☎ 366 6612 ⏰ Daily lunch, dinner

HARBOUR CLUB (€€)

You can't help but notice the 'Harbour' monopoly on Kyrenia's waterfront—a café, pizzeria, bar and restaurant, and they all offer the same menu of international and Turkish-Cypriot dishes. This has alfresco seating.

🚺 J3 ✉ Kyrenia Harbour ☎ 815 2211 🕐 Daily lunch, dinner

LAGOON SEAFOOD RESTAURANT (€€)

www.niazis.com
Select your seafood from the display, let the waiter know how you'd like it, then prepare for some of the freshest seafood you'll find in the north.

🚺 J3 ✉ Kordonboyu Caddesi, Kyrenia ☎ 815 6555 🕐 Daily lunch, dinner

LAUGHING BUDDHA (€€)

Expats swear this is the most authentic Chinese in the north, but they also come for the warm welcome and atmosphere.

🚺 J3 ✉ Ecevit Caddesi, Kyrenia ☎ 815 8715 🕐 Daily lunch, dinner

LEMON TREE (€)

This longstanding local favourite is justifiably popular for its tasty meze and fresh seafood.

🚺 J4 ✉ Catalköy Road, east of Kyrenia ☎ 824 4045 🕐 Daily lunch, dinner

MIRAGE (€€)

www.niazis.com
Expect Turkish-Cypriot dishes and international bistro food at this chic but casual café-bar. Having only recently opened, it is rapidly becoming *the* place to go among locals.

🚺 J3 ✉ Gonyeli Cadessi, Nicosia ☎ 223 8888 🕐 Daily lunch, dinner

MISSINA (€€)

Most head to this elegant restaurant for its seaside location, but the seafood here is outstanding. There's also a popular buffet but fresh is always best. Book a table.

🚺 J3 ✉ 16 Omer Faydali Sokak, Karaoglanoglu, near Kyrenia ☎ 822 3844 🕐 Daily lunch, dinner

NIAZI'S (€)

www.niazis.com
One of Kyrenia's most popular restaurants,

'FULL KEBAB'

Nothing defines the northern Cypriot dining experience more than the 'full kebab'. A combination of Turkish and Cypriot specialties, it consists of a series of grilled meats, along with accompaniments such as dips and salads. The meats, such as meatballs, kebabs, chops and *kofta* (minced kebab meat) are served as they're ready, each fresh off the grill and timed to coincide with the last course being finished. To enjoy the experience fully, arrive hungry and order some local red wine.

locals and expats come regularly for the famous 'full kebab'. Expect course after course of delicious grilled meats to be brought to your table—chops, sausages, *kofta* and more—all slightly charred and smoky yet succulent inside. Best not to eat that day in preparation for what will be a very filling meal. The open fire where the meat is grilled makes this a cosy winter spot.

🚺 J3 ✉ Opposite Dome Hotel, Kyrenia Harbour ☎ 815 2160 🕐 Daily dinner only

PASHA (€)

A family run restaurant set in a traditional village house. The menu is limited but you can't beat it for authentic, typically Turkish snacks and meals, including *lahmacum* (Turkish pizza) or *manti* (dumplings). Enjoy with Turkish tea.

🚺 J4 ✉ Village centre, Belapais ☎ 838 7070 🕐 Daily lunch, dinner

EL SABOR LATINO (€)

You'll either find this modern décor in the heart of old Nicosia disconcerting or refreshing, but most agree the menu of Spanish, Italian and even Mexican cuisine is a welcome change from the usual 'full kebab' experience or expat staples.

🚺 b2 ✉ 29 Selimiye Square, Nicosia ☎ 228 8322 🕐 Daily lunch, dinner

Where to Stay

Hotels and resorts dot the island every-where from the big towns to remote areas. Expect everything from modest hotels where the beachside setting is the attraction to five-star luxury resorts with fine restaurants and stylish spas.

Introduction

Cyprus has a bewildering number of hotels and resorts. Most take advantage of the splendid coastline and are focused on keeping guests happy as they soak up the brilliant sunny weather. As a result, there is a large number of massive resorts that might lack personality and the personal touch, but they offer an array of amenities, from spas to sailing.

What to Expect

You'll mostly find four- and five-star properties on Cyprus, with a smattering of three-stars, with comfort and amenity levels in line with what you would expect on mainland Europe. Price categories are divided into high season and low season and many beach resorts and hotels will close over winter, opening again in March or April after a spring clean. At the four- and five-stars you can expect a swimming pool, beach access with sun beds, and water-based activities such as diving or sail boarding. Remember to book well in advance for summer.

Eating, Drinking and Self-Catering

There is usually a beach or pool bar, casual dining options and a more formal restaurant. Breakfasts are nearly always buffets (including hot items such as eggs) and hotels are generally in tune with their guests needs. Full- or half-board options are fine if you're in an area where you need a car to drive to town, but the same menu can get tiresome after a few days. Many resorts offer apartments or bungalows that have mini kitchens for self-catering and are fine for preparing simple meals.

LOCATION, LOCATION, LOCATION

Nothing is far away on Cyprus, so no matter where you are if you have a car you can easily get around. Location becomes important when it comes to eating and entertainment. If you're a foodie, opt for Limassol or Larnaka. If you want to soak up the local culture and café scene, try Nicosia. Wanting to meet other tourists? Then maybe Agia Napa is more your scene.

Take your pick—from modern apartments and small hotels to luxurious resort hotels and mountain retreats

PRICES

Expect to pay under €100/190YTL per night for a double room in a budget hotel.

Southern Cyprus
AGAPINOR

www.agapinorhotel.com.cy
A typical old-fashioned Cyprus holiday hotel, the Agapinor is comfortable and well appointed with excellent views. Swimming pool.
⊞ C8 ⊠ 24–28 Odos Nikodimou Mylona, Pafos ☎ 2693 3926

BUNCH OF GRAPES INN

High in the quaint village of Pissouri, this simple, rustic old inn gives guests a sample of village life. With only 11 rooms set around a simple courtyard, it is very peaceful.
⊞ E8 ⊠ 9 Odos Ioannou Erotokritou, Pissouri village ☎ 2522 1275

CENTRUM

www.centrumhotel.net
Right in the heart of the atmospheric old town, this hotel has a stylish foyer and bar. While the rooms aren't as flashy as the public areas, it's still great value. Free Wi-Fi.
⊞ b3 ⊠ 15 Odos Pasikratous, Eleftherias Square, Nicosia ☎ 2245 6444

CURIUM PALACE

www.curiumpalace.com
This elegant 1950s hotel has been updated, with a satisfying mix of original fittings and fixtures and modern touches. The 63 rooms are all modern, the staff are charming and the food notable.
⊞ G8 ⊠ 11 Odos Lordou Vyronou, Limassol ☎ 2589 1100

LATCHI HOTEL

www.latchihotel.com
Overlooking Latchi Harbour, this hotel, situated in a handsome stone building, is only 50m (55 yards) from the local pebble beach. The rooms are basic but clean and well maintained and the hotel's wonderful harbourside restaurant is enticing.
⊞ C6 ⊠ Leoforos Akamandos, Latchi ☎ 2632 1411

SUN HALL HOTEL

www.sunhallhotel-24.com
Right on the town beach promenade, this hotel and apartment complex (good for families) is well situated for discovering old Larnaka. There is a range of services and facilities, including a

BACKPACKER BLUES

Unlike the Greek Islands, Cyprus doesn't really cater for the backpacker, as it's seen as a holiday spot for families and wealthier older visitors. While there is a breed of new 'hipper' resorts on the island, it still has a dearth of low-budget options.

decent swimming pool, which make this a good-value option.
⊞ L7 ⊠ 6 Leoforos Athinon, Larnaka ☎ 2465 3341

Northern Cyprus
DELCRAFT

www.ecotourismcyprus.com
Cyprus' first eco-village offers cozy lodgings in a restored stone house. The traditional village atmosphere is the drawcard, as are activities such as olive-picking, bread-baking and walks with local shepherds.
⊞ N3 ⊠ Büyükkonuk village, Karpaz Peninsula ☎ 383 2038

KARPAZ ARCH HOUSES

www.karpazarchhouses.com
There is charm galore at the arch houses, set in an old renovated stone building. The small village is close to the brilliant beaches of the Karpaz Peninsula and all rooms have A/C, fridges and cooking facilities.
⊞ Q1 ⊠ Dipkarpaz village ☎ 372 2009

NOSTALGIA HOTEL

www.nostalgia-boutiquehotel.com
This small hotel in a stone building has plenty of charm in its 28 individually decorated rooms. Centrally located and with good facilities (including swimming pool), it's excellent value.
⊞ J3 ⊠ 22 Cafer Pasa Sokak, Kyrenia ☎ 815 3079

Mid-Range Hotels

Southern Cyprus
ATLANTICA BAY
www.atlanticahotels.com
With commanding
views over Limassol Bay
and close to ancient
Amathous, this is a good
reason to stay out of
the heart of Limassol.
The rooms are well
appointed—sea-facing are
more romantic—and there
are plenty of water-based
activities on offer.
➕ G8 ✉ Leoforos Amathous,
Limassol ☎ 2563 4070

ATLANTICA
MIRAMARE BEACH
www.atlanticahotels.com
Located just outside of
Limassol, this long-standing favourite (especially
with loyal British visitors)
has been renovated, mak-
ing it more enticing than
ever. Extensive facilities, a
quiet location and excel-
lent service.
➕ G8 ✉ Odos Amerikanas,
Potamos Germasogeias
☎ 2588 8100

CALLISTO HOLIDAY
VILLAGE
www.aquasolhotels.com
This Greek-style family
focused apartment com-
plex on the beach offers
lots of activities and there
are several swimming

pools. Accommodation
comes with kitchenettes,
although there are a
couple of kid-friendly
restaurants and bars on
site as well.
➕ N6 ✉ Leoforos
Amathousm, Ayia Napa
☎ 2372 4500

COLUMBIA BEACH
HOTEL
www.columbia-hotels.com
While less lavish than the
sister resort next door, the
Columbia Hotel is still a
fine option, with extensive
amenities, an elegant bar
and a lovely pool area.
Full sea-view rooms are
wonderful and the staff
are warm and welcoming.
➕ E9 ✉ Pissouri Beach,
Pissouri ☎ 2583 3333

CYPRUS
AGROTOURISM
www.agrotourism.com.cy
The Cyprus Agrotourism

Company has a long list
of charming stone houses
on their books in the
areas of Larnaka, Nicosia,
Limassol and Pafos that
are ideal for self-catering
holidays. Many of the
houses are in a traditional
style, often two storey,
with shady verandas, leafy
gardens and swimming
pools. They are set either
in or around delightful
villages or in the picturesque countryside.
➕ Off map at C5 ✉ 19
Leoforos Lemesou, Nicosia
☎ 2234 0071

HOLIDAY INN
www.ichotelgroup.com
A good choice in the old
city; you'll find it a decent
hotel if you get one of
the refurbished rooms.
While the breakfasts are
average for a hotel of this
standard, the Italian restaurant serves excellent
pizzas and pastas.
➕ a3 ✉ 70 Odos Regaena,
Nicosia ☎ 2271 2712

LOUIS PRINCESS
BEACH
www.louishotels.com
Fully refurbished for
summer 2008, this
perennial favourite now
has even more to recom-
mend it. From the long
sand beach to stylishly
renovated rooms (the
sea-view rooms are worth
the money) curving
around the lagoon-style
pool, it's a hotel that
encourages you to have
an outdoor lifestyle.
➕ L7 ✉ Dekeleia Road,

6km (3.5 miles) from Larnaka
☎ 2464 5500

MEDITERRANEAN BEACH

www.medbeach.com
With its recent revamp, and right on a blue-flag beach, this hotel is a desirable place along this crowded stretch. Extensive facilities including swimming pools, spa, water sports, gym, and vast public spaces, make it a good family choice.
➕ L7 ✉ Leoforos Amathous, Larnaka ☎ 2531 1777

MILL HOTEL

www.cymillhotel.com
This family-owned hotel is one of the best reasons to visit Kakopetria. A former mill, it turns on the charm with its spacious rooms, views over the old town, and a delightful rustic restaurant on the upper level.
➕ F6 ✉ 8 Milos, Kakopetria
☎ 2292 2536

NISSI BEACH RESORT

www.hotelsayianapa.com
On a wonderful bay that features a 500m (550 yards) beach (with reserved sun beds for guests), this is a classic Agia summer resort, complete with beach bungalows. With a good-sized pool, lovely gardens and plenty of dining options, it's easy to stay focused on your tan and holiday reading.
➕ N6 ✉ Leoforos Nissi, Agia Napa ☎ 2372 1021

Northern Cyprus
BELLAPAIS GARDENS

www.bellapaisgardens.com
Peacefully perched on the slopes of Belapais, this is the best and most charming of the hotels in the area. The luxurious duplex-style apartments afford privacy and there is a lovely swimming pool and a fine restaurant with brilliant views.
➕ J4 ✉ Crusader Road, Belapais ☎ 815 6066

DOME HOTEL

To be recommended, with an unbeatable position on its own rocky outcrop just around from the harbour, this long-standing hotel is something of an institution. And while it does have a slightly institutional feel (especially at meal times), it retains enough

old-school charm. Brilliant views and pool.
➕ J3 ✉ Kordonboyu, Kyrenia ☎ 815 2453

ROCKS HOTEL & CASINO

www.rockshotel.com
In a good spot not far from the harbour, the superior room standards, complete with a 'maxi' bar as well as a mini bar, make the Rocks Hotel a safe bet. The hotel has an English pub and the obligatory casino.
➕ J3 ✉ Kordonboyu, Kyrenia ☎ 815 2238

SALAMIS BAY CONTI RESORT

www.salamisbayconti.com
A massive lagoon-style swimming pool and a pristine private beach on Salamis Bay hint at what the focus is at this upmarket resort. As well as the usual standard hotel rooms, there are bungalows that sleep five to six people.
➕ N5 ✉ Salamis Bay, near Famagusta ☎ 378 8200

SARAY

This side of the Green Line has a hotel vacuum, however, the Saray is the mainstay of business travellers and visitors to the capital. Spotless rooms, some with interesting views from their tiny balconies, and good service set this hotel apart—casino excepted, of course.
➕ Off map at c1 ✉ Atatürk Meydani, Nicosia ☎ 228 3115

Luxury Hotels

PRICES

Expect to pay over €180/345YTL per night for a double room in a luxury hotel.

Southern Cyprus
ALMYRA

www.thanoshotels.com
You can rest easy at the Almyra knowing that you're staying in the best resort in town. With its stylish public areas, sophisticated cuisine and modish style, it's surprising that it's also a very family friendly resort. The Kyma Suites, which boast rooftop terraces, are wonderful.
➕ C8 ✉ Poseidonos, Pafos ☎ 2688 8700

ANASSA

www.thanoshotels.com
A luxurious and expansive Mediterranean-style resort, with generously sized rooms, beautiful landscaped gardens and a wonderful pool area. The brilliant views of the Akamas Peninsula are the icing on a very fine cake. The restaurants are highly regarded and there is a noteworthy spa.
➕ C6 ✉ Polis Beach, Polis, near Pafos ☎ 2688 8000

APHRODITE HILLS

www.aphroditehills.com
This contemporary InterContinental property has 290 generously sized rooms, all with balconies. As it's not on the beach (although it has a beach club), the excellent 18-hole golf course and massive spa are the main attractions.
➕ D8 ✉ Aphrodite Hills, Petra tou Romiou, near Kouklia ☎ 2682 8000

COLUMBIA BEACH RESORT

www.columbia-hotels.com
The pick of the Pissouri Bay properties, this resort has palpable Mediterranean charm. A great place to unwind, the massive swimming pool, beautiful beach, exceptional spa and excellent restaurants might see you not leave the property for the duration of your stay—certainly nothing to be ashamed of.
➕ E9 ✉ Pissouri Bay ☎ 2583 3000

FOUR SEASONS

The best run luxury resort on the island, this Four Seasons might not be part of the Four Seasons group, but it does a great job of reaching the same heights of service. The rooms are spacious, luxurious, and have amazing amenities, the restaurants are serving the most refined food on the island, and the pool, public areas and spa are all first class. Return guests—and they have many—are treated like royalty.
✉ Leoforos Amathous, Limassol ☎ 2585 8000; www.fourseasons.com.cy

LONDA

www.londahotel.com
The hippest hotel in town is sleek and boutique, with Italian style and effortless cool from the popular bar to the thoughtfully designed suites. Within splashing distance of the sea are a stunning pool area and a great restaurant.
➕ G8 ✉ 72 Georgiou I, Limassol ☎ 2586 5555

LE MÉRIDIEN LIMASSOL SPA & RESORT

www.lemeridien-cyprus.com
This vast hotel with over 300 rooms still manages to sate the whims of the guests with an expansive array of amenities, including a huge spa. Plenty of poolside space (and several pools), restaurants and bars take guests' minds off the out of the way location.
➕ G8 ✉ Old Limassol–Nicosia Road, Limassol ☎ 2586 2000

Northern Cyprus
THE COLONY HOTEL

www.thecolonycyprus.com
An elegant hotel, probably the most atmospheric property in Kyrenia. From comfortable club rooms to enormous two-bedroom suites, it has oodles of old-world charm and service to match.
➕ J3 ✉ Ecevit Caddesi, Kyrenia ☎ 815 1518

Need to Know

This section offers all the practical details you'll need to know about Cyprus, from when to go and how to get there to how to get around when you're there, as well as opening hours, language, useful websites and other helpful information.

Planning Ahead

When to Go

Cyprus is generally a summer destination and bulges at the seams during July and August. Try to avoid the height of summer madness and go during the shoulder seasons (Apr–May and Sep–Oct) for a mix of milder temperatures and open facilities; most beach amenities are closed in winter.

TIME

L Cyprus is two hours ahead of GMT except from the end of March to the end of October when it's three hours.

AVERAGE DAILY MAXIMUM TEMPERATURES

JAN	FEB	MAR	APR	MAY	JUN	JUL	AUG	SEP	OCT	NOV	DEC
62°F	62°F	66°F	73°F	79°F	86°F	89°F	90°F	88°F	81°F	72°F	66°F
17°C	17°C	19°C	23°C	26°C	30°C	32°C	33°C	31°C	27°C	22°C	19°C

Spring (March to May) has a mix of sunshine and showers, increasingly clear toward the summer months.
Summer (June to August) is hot and dry with rarely any respite and little chance of rain.
Autumn (September to November) waters are still warm at the end of summer, but there is an increasing chance of bad weather toward the winter season.
Winter (December to February) brings a mix of heavy rain and mild temperatures, and snow in the mountains.

WHAT'S ON

January *Epiphany* (6 Jan): Important Greek Orthodox religious celebration.
February/March *Carnival* (60 days before Easter): This 10-day celebration marks the beginning of Lent.
April *National Day* (1 Apr): Celebrates the EOKA uprising for self-determination.
National Sovereignty and Turkish Children's Festival (23 Apr).
April/May Celebrations surrounding Orthodox Easter are the biggest of the calendar and generally fall in mid–late April to early May.
May *May Fair in Pafos* (1 May): A ten-day fair of cultural events, flora and local craft exhibitions.

Anthestiria Flower Festival (early May): Celebrates everything good about spring, centred in Pafos.
Turkish Youth Festival (19 May).
Cyprus International Fair (late May): The Island's biggest trade fair.
July *Larnaka Festival* (all month): Theatre and dance events.
Peace and Freedom Day (20 Jul): A holiday in the north celebrating Turkish intervention in 1974.
August/September *Turkish Communal Resistance Day* (1 Aug).
Turkish Victory Day (30 Aug).
Limassol Wine Festival (late Aug–early Sep): A 12-day

festival celebrating harvest with music and dance.
October *Independence Day* (1 Oct).
Greek National Day (28 Oct): Known as 'Ohi' (No) day, it's a day of parades in the south. This refers to a day in 1940 when Italy's Mussolini (who wished to use Greek sites to fight the Allies) gave the Greek Metaxas dictatorship an ultimatum. Metaxas responded with a simple, 'no'.
Turkish National Day (29 Oct).
November *Proclamation of Turkish Republic of Northern Cyprus* (15 Nov).

Cyprus Online
www.visitcyprus.com
The official portal of the southern Cyprus Tourist Organisation, it's packed full of useful information for pre-planning your trip. The site has UK, US, International and Greek versions.

www.northcyprus.cc
This is the official website for the northern Cyprus Tourism Centre. There's loads of information on accommodation, activities, events and festivals.

www.cyprusnet.com
This massive Cyprus portal has links to every conceivable website on Cyprus, including hotel and apartment rental sites, travel agencies, real estate agencies, Cyprus media, car hire, along with handy information such as the weather and exchange rates.

www.cyprus-art.com
The Cyprus Cultural Informer is a 'what's on' website with information on latest events, film screenings, concerts, plays and even dance parties. It seems to be sporadically updated.

www.windowoncyprus.com
It may not be the most professional looking site around, but it's certainly comprehensive, offering an enormous portal with links to lots of other useful information.

www.northcyprus.net
The northern Cyprus Hotelier's Association website has a search engine so you can search for accommodation in the areas you're interested in staying. It's the most comprehensive northern Cyprus hotel site.

www.cyprus-agrotourism.com
If you fancy spending a holiday chilling out in a charming traditional stone farmhouse, then head to this booking site, which has the most comprehensive listings.

PRIME TRAVEL SITES
www.bookcyprus.com
A Cyprus-based accommodation booking site; many travellers claim they offer the best rates and there are lots of great last-minute deals.

www.ornekholidays.com
This is the site for northern Cyprus's biggest and best travel agency; you can book everything here from birdwatching holidays to diving courses, along with hotels, car hire and guides.

INTERNET ACCESS
You'll find internet cafés in most cities in southern and northern Cyprus, while good hotels will offer wireless access in hotel rooms, a business centre on the property, or at worst a computer in the lobby that you can use.

Getting There

ENTRY REQUIREMENTS

A passport valid for six months past the entry point is required for most countries (some national ID cards are accepted) for a stay of up to 90 days. Pre-arranged visas are not required for visitors from most countries. When crossing into the north from the south or if arriving at Ercan airport, you will receive your immigration entry stamp on a separate piece of paper.

INSURANCE

Travel insurance is always a good idea whenever you travel, but is not strictly required to enter either the south or the north. In the south, reduced-cost emergency medical treatment is provided to people from other EU member states with the EHIC card, however, this is no substitute for adequate travel insurance.
Although unlikely, if you have permission from the hire car company to take a rental car from the south to the north, you are required to take out extra insurance that can be purchased at the Ledra Street border crossing.

AIRPORTS

South Cyprus has two main international airports, Larnaka and Pafos, and both host regular direct flights from Europe and the Middle East. Ercan Airport is the main international airport in the north, although charter flights also arrive at Gecitkale Airport near Famagusta.

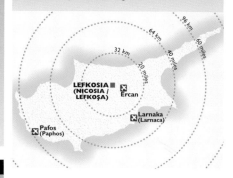

FROM LARNAKA INTERNATIONAL AIRPORT

Larnaka's International Airport (☎ 2481 6426; www.hermesairports.com), only 5km (3 miles) from the city centre, is the island's more senior international stop and has been expanded to include a new terminal. While it's fine to take a taxi to the city from this airport, if you're travelling further it's most economical and convenient to have either organized a rental car pick-up or a transfer from your hotel as a taxi transfer can cost as much as a day's car rental.

FROM PAFOS INTERNATIONAL AIRPORT

Pafos International Airport (☎ 2481 6426; www.hermesairports.com) is 10km (6 miles) from the city and is exceptionally busy during summer high season. A taxi, transfer or car hire is the usual means of transportation to or from the airport.

FROM NORTHERN CYPRUS AIRPORTS

The main airport in northern Cyprus is Ercan Airport (☎ 231 4806). Nicosia (23km/14 miles), Kyrenia (35km/21 miles) and Famagusta (50km/31 miles) are easily reached

from here by taxi. While there are regular charter flights to Ercan, commercial flights must touchdown on mainland Turkey before continuing on to northern Cyprus. Istanbul, Izmir, Ankara, Adana and Antalya are the most common stops on the mainland.

ARRIVING BY FERRY

You can arrive in Cyprus via ferry at ports in the north and south. In the south, the main ferry terminal is at Limassol and is mainly serviced by ferries from Rhodes and Ayios Nikolaos in Crete. In the north there are ferry terminals at Famagusta and Kyrenia with connections to mainland Turkey cities such as Mersin, Alanya, Antalya and Tasucu.

NORTH VERSUS SOUTH

The frost is certainly thawing between the north and south, however, a trip to Cyprus that includes a visit to both points of the compass was still problematic at the time of research. If you arrive in the south, you can cross at the Ledra crossing where you will have to show your passport on the Greek-Cypriot side then walk across the buffer zone known as the Green Line (the UN-patrolled no-man's land) to the Turkish-Cypriot side where you will get entry stamps on a separate piece of paper. When returning you'll receive another stamp on the Turkish-Cypriot side and will then be asked some questions on the Greek-Cypriot side, where you'll more than likely have your bags searched. By law, you are not allowed to take any products from the north to the south. If arriving at Ercan Airport in the north you are officially not allowed to enter into the south, however, at the time of research all of this was up in the air as steps were being taken toward unification.

Note: at the time of writing the UK does not recognize the self-declared Turkish Republic of Northern Cyprus (TRNC). For updated information on developments refer to the British Foreign Office website at www.fco.gov.uk.

CUSTOMS LIMITS

● **Republic of Cyprus:**
EU nationals do not have to declare goods imported for personal use. The limits for visitors arriving from outside the EU are as follows: Alcohol (over 22% vol) 1L; wine 2L; sparkling or fortified wine 2L; beer 110L; cigarettes 200 or cigarillos 100 or cigars 50; tobacco 250g; perfume 50g

● **Northern Cyprus:**
Alcohol (over 22% vol) 1L; wine 1.5L; cigarettes 400 or cigarillos 200 or cigars 100; tobacco 1kg; perfume 100ml

TOURIST OFFICES

Southern Cyprus: Cyprus Tourism Organisation
● Nicosia ✉ Odos Aristokyprou, Laiki Geitonia ☎ 2267 4264
● Limassol ✉ 115A Odos Spyrou Araouzou ☎ 2536 2756
● Larnaka ✉ Plateia Vasileos Pavlou ☎ 2465 4322
● Pafos ✉ 3 Odos Gladstonos ☎ 2693 2841
Agia Napa ✉ 12 Leoforos
Northern Cyprus:
● Nicosia ✉ Kyrenia Gate ☎ 228 9629
● Kyrenia ✉ Kyrenia Harbour ☎ 815 2145
● Famagusta ✉ Akkule ☎ 366 2864

Getting Around

VISITORS WITH DISABILITIES

For those with disabilities, Cyprus can be a difficult destination as there are very few disabled-friendly facilities, apart from a few hotels being equipped with disabled rooms. Outside the major cities, villages and towns have many uneven or broken pavements—if they're there at all.

BOAT TRIPS

There are one-day boat excursions from Limassol Harbour to Lady's Mile Beach; Pafos Harbour to Coral Bay and Agios Georgios; Agia Napa to Paralimni and Protaras; Larnaka Marina along Larnaka, Agia Napa and Protaras coast; and Lakki along the Akamas coast. These operate during the tourist season only. In the north, there are boat trips from Kyrenia Harbour to the beaches of Acapulco or Mare Monte during the warmer months. A number of companies also operate excellent catamaran cruises, which can be very relaxing. See Enter-tainment and Activities in the regional sections for further information.

How you get around the island depends entirely on how you wish to spend your time in Cyprus. If you simply want to lie in the sun and leaf through magazines, your airport transfer may be the last form of transport you take until you leave for the airport again. If you wish to explore the island, either north or south, it's best to hire a car, as local bus services are tailored more toward local needs rather than those of visitors, especially in the north. There are service taxis (that ply predetermined routes), however, they're very slow and once again aimed at locals; they generally stop running around 6pm. Within cities there are buses that service the city centre—ask the tourist office or your hotel concierge for a timetable. You'll also find timetables on signs handily placed next to beachside bus stops.

CAR HIRE

● An overwhelming number of visitors to Cyprus choose to hire a car, generally making arrangements before their trip (often as part of a package deal), picking up the car from the airport upon arrival and returning it there on departure. The good news though is that even if you planned on a beach holiday but get the urge to take a drive once you arrive, hire cars are cheap and plentiful on the island, and the roads are fine. In fact the island is excellent to explore, whether heading between cities, taking the backroads through the mountains or beach hopping.

● Vehicle rental is common and easy in Cyprus—in both north and south. Most of the international companies are represented (Budget, Avis, Europcar), as well as there being a wealth of local rental companies located at every tourist hotspot on the island offering everything from scooters to large 4WDs. Rates are in line with, if not a little cheaper than, continental European rates, but the vehicles are sometimes a little scruffy.

● If you want to go with an international company, it's much cheaper to organize the vehicle

in advance. Note that with some companies, an international driving license will be required—ask before you book.

● If you're planning on heading into the mountains, a vehicle with adequate power to tackle the steep sections is advisable. If you're heading for the mountains during winter a 4WD is a wise idea as the weather can change quickly. Also, the dirt roads you'll encounter if you're exploring some of the more remote beaches are better suited to a 4WD.

DRIVING TIPS
● Drive on the left.
● Speed limits: on motorways and dual carriageways 100kph/62mph; minimum 65kph/40mph (northern Cyprus 60mph/37mph); country roads 80kph/49mph (northern Cyprus 40mph/26pmh); urban roads 50kph/31mph, or as signposted (northern Cyprus 30kph/18mph).
● Seatbelts must be worn at all times, if fitted.
● There is random breath testing—never drive under the influence of alcohol.
● Fuel is slightly less expensive on the island than it is in Europe. Fuel stations in the north are open until around 9pm, while in the south they're generally open 6am-6pm, but have credit card or cash vending machines operating at other times.
● In the south, the Cyprus Automobile Association in Nicosia (☎ 2231 3131) has a 24-hour breakdown service affiliated with the Alliance International de Tourisme (AIT). If you have a rental car follow the instructions in your documentation.

TAXIS
Taxis are plentiful in the cities and larger towns. As a visitor you won't have any problems finding one, as they will generally find you. Always make sure that the meter is on or negotiate a fare first. The majority of drivers will have good knowlege of the more popular tourist destinations.

PLACE NAMES
It's worth noting that different names of destinations—in Greek, Turkish or English—can cause confusion, especially since the signage on the roads is not always consistent. Limassol for instance is sometimes signposted as Lemesos, while Lefkosia, Lefkoşa and Nicosia are all the same place, Kyrenia is the same as Keryneia or Girne, and so on. Obviously, place names are political in Cyprus. In the text and on the maps, we have tried to reflect as many of the varied spellings or names as possible. On the ground in the south, street names can also be inconsistent—Greek or anglicized. The following translations might help: *plateia* means square; *odos* means street/road; *leoforos* means avenue.

YOUTH HOSTELS
Cyprus isn't really on the backpacker trail, but there are youth hostels (www.hostelcyprus.com) around the island and the 'Euro<26' card will give cardholders discounts on a wide range of services. The Cyprus Youth Board (☎ 2240 2600; www.youthboard.org.cy) can provide more information.

Essential Facts

TIPPING

● Hotels, restaurants, café's and bars all have a 10 per cent surcharge built into the bill. Porters, taxi drivers and tour guides generally expect a small tip.

MONEY

● The Euro (€) is now the official currency of southern Cyprus. In the north, the currency is the New Turkish Lira (YTL).

EMERGENCY NUMBERS

● Police: 112 (south); 155 (north)
● Fire: 112 (south); 199 (north)
● Ambulance: 112 (south); 112 (north)

ELECTRICITY

● The power supply is 240 volts and the type of socket is generally a European two round pin style, but there are some older buildings with UK-style three rectangular pins.

HEALTH AND SAFETY

● Sun Advice: Cyprus enjoys near perfect weather outside the winter months, so staying in the sun too long without adequate protection can be a problem and can ruin a holiday. Wear a hat, use a high-protection sunscreen and have plenty of fluids on hand—non-alcoholic fluids.

● Medicines: minor ailments can be dealt with at pharmacies (*farmakio* in the south, *eczane* in the north). Most pharmacists speak English and many medicines that require a prescription elsewhere are available over the counter.

● Safe Water: tap water is generally safe to drink, but for some travellers it doesn't take much to initiate an upset stomach. If you are in any doubt, it is best to stick to bottled water that has either been opened in front of you or purchased by you.

● Personal Safety: the police in Cyprus are helpful and English is generally widely spoken. Crime is at a reassuringly low level, but take the usual precautions with regard to handbags and items left in vehicles—especially as rental cars are easily spotted by their red number-plates. Keep in mind that there are many military areas on both sides of the island and it's important to keep an eye on road signs that indicate military areas. Photographing anything vaguely military will cause problems.

NATIONAL HOLIDAYS

● 1 Jan: New Years Day; 6 Jan: Epiphany (south); 25 Mar: Greek National Day (south); 1 Apr: Cyprus National Day (south); 23 Apr: Children's Day (National Sovereignty Day, north); Apr/May: Orthodox Easter (south); 1 May: Labour Day; 19 May: Youth and Sports Day (north); May/Jun: Pentecost/Kataklysmos (Festival of the Flood, south); 20 Jul: Peace and

Freedom Day (north); 15 Aug: Assumption of Our Lady (south); 30 Aug: Victory Day (north); 1 Oct: Cyprus Independence Day (south); 28 Oct: Greek National ('Ohi') Day (south); 29 Oct: Turkish National Day (north); 15 Nov: Independence Day (north); 25–26 Dec: Christmas–Boxing Day (south).

OPENING HOURS

In Cyprus, opening hours are vague guidelines that can be either hazy numbers or just treated with disdain. While this can be frustrating, learn to go with the Mediterranean flow. During summer shops are generally open longer at night.

● SOUTH:

Shops: Mon–Fri 9am–1.30pm, 4–6.30pm (closed Wed, Sat pm).
Banks: Mon–Fri 9am–12.30pm (some branches open in the afternoon).
Museums: Tue–Sat 9am–5pm, Sun 9am–1pm.
Archaeological sites: major 9am–4pm, until 5pm summer; minor 9am–3pm, often closed on weekends or Mon.
Restaurants: noon–4pm, 6pm–late (depending on season).

● NORTH:

Shops: summer Mon–Fri 8am–1pm, 4–7pm (closed Sat pm), winter 9am–1pm, 2–6pm (closed Sat pm).
Banks: Mon–Fri 9am–12.30pm (some branches open in the afternoon).
Museums and archaeological sites: summer 9am–6pm (some close weekends), winter 9am–1pm, 2–4.45pm.
Restaurants: noon–4pm, 6pm–late (depending on season).

TELEPHONES

● Phone Cards for public phone boxes and mobile phones are sold in kiosks all over the island and are generally available in €5, €10, €20 and €50 units.
● International Dialling Codes: UK 00 44; USA 00 1; Netherlands 00 31; Spain 00 34; Germany 00 49

EMBASSIES AND CONSULATES

● UK
South ✉ Odos Alexander Pallis, Nicosia ☎ 2286 1100
North ✉ Leoforos Shakespeare, 29 Mehmet Akif Cad, Nicosia ☎ 228 3861
● Germany
South ✉ 10 Odos Nikitaras, 1080 Nicosia ☎ 2245 1145
North ✉ No 15, 28 Odos Kasım, Nicosia ☎ 227 5161
● USA
South ✉ Odos Metochiou and Ploutarchou 2407, Engomi, Nicosia ☎ 2239 3939
North ✉ 6 Serif Arzik Sokak, Nicosia ☎ 227 3930 or 2266 9965 from south Cyprus
● Netherlands
South ✉ 34 Leoforos Demosthenis Severis, Nicosia ☎ 2287 3666
● Spain
South ✉ 4th floor, 32 Leoforos Strovolos, Nicosia ☎ 2245 0410

Language

Greek is spoken in the Republic of Cyprus and Turkish in the north. Most Greek Cypriots are quite fluent in English but in some rural towns and villages locals might not know any English so an attempt at the language would be useful. In the North things are very different; some basic words in Turkish is an advantage as most of the Turkish Cypriots have a limited knowledge of English. Here are some words and phrases that you may find helpful.

USEFUL WORDS AND PHRASES

ENGLISH	GREEK	TURKISH
yes	*ne*	*evet*
no	*óhi*	*hoyir*
please	*parakaló*	*lütfen*
thank you	*efcharistó*	*tesekkür ederim*
hello	*yásas, yásoo*	*merhaba*
goodbye	*yásas, yásoo*	*hosça kal*
sorry	*signómi*	*özür delerim*
how much?	*póso?*	*ne kadar?*
I (don't) understand	*(dhen) katalavéno*	*sizi anliyorum*

MONEY

bank	*trápeza*	*banka*
exchange office	*ghrafío sinalághmatos*	*kambiyo bürosu*
post office	*tahidhromío*	*postane*
money	*leftá*	*para*
cash desk	*tamío*	*kasa*
credit card	*pistotikí kárta*	*kredi karti*
traveller's cheque	*taxidhyoikí epitayí*	*seyahat çeki*
exchange rate	*isotimía*	*döviz kuru*

TRANSPORT

ENGLISH	GREEK	TURKISH
aeroplane	*aeropláno*	*uçak*
airport	*aerodhrómio*	*havaalani*
bus	*leoforío*	*otobüs*
...station	*...stathmós*	*...otogar*
boat	*karávi*	*gemi vapur*
...port	*...limáni*	*...liman*
ticket	*isitírio*	*bilet*
...single/return	*...apló metepistrofís*	*...tek gidis/gidis dönüs*

ACCOMMODATION

hotel	*xenodhohío*	*otel*
room	*dhomátyo*	*oda*
single/double	*monó/dhipló*	*tek/iki kishilik*
breakfast	*proinó*	*kahvalti*
toilet	*twaléta*	*tuvalet*
bath	*bányo*	*banyo*
shower	*doos*	*dus*
balcony	*balkóni*	*balkon*

EATING OUT

restaurant	*estiatório*	*restoran*
café	*kafenío*	*kafeterya*
menu	*menóo*	*menü*
lunch	*yévma*	*öglc ycmcgi*
dinner	*dhípno*	*aksam yemegi*
dessert	*epidhórpyo*	*tatli*
waiter	*garsóni*	*garson*
the bill	*loghariazmós*	*hesap*

Timeline

9000–3800BC First migrants arrive from Asia Minor.

2500–1050BC Bronze Age settlers arrive from the eastern Mediterranean.

700BC Assyria claims control of Cyprus.

570BC Egyptian pharaoh Amasis becomes effective ruler of Cyprus.

545BC Cyprus submits to Persian rule.

325–58BC Hellenistic Period: Greek controlled Cyprus embraces Greek culture.

58BC–AD330 Romans rule and great amphitheatres, baths and temples are built.

330–395 The Roman Empire splits and the Byzantine era begins.

7th and 10th centuries Arab raids weaken Byzantine control.

1191 Richard the Lionheart, enroute to the Holy Land, conquers Cyprus.

1192–1489 Lusignan rule. The Latin cathedrals of Nicosia and Famagusta are built.

1489 Venetians, invited to combat the troublesome Genoese, take the island themselves.

1571 Ottoman Turks take control of Cyprus.

Left to right: an armoured statue in the Cyprus Museum, Nicosia; mosaic floor in the House of Dionysos, Pafos; main tracery window on the Lala Mustafa Paşa Mosque, Famagusta; UN vehicles patrol the Green Line, Nicosia; frescoes decorating Asinou Church; the Lion of Venice standing guard outside the Cyprus Museum, Nicosia

1878 Britain, in agreement with Turkey, takes control.

1914 Britain formally annexes Cyprus as Turkey fights for Germany in WWI.

1955 EOKA (Ethniki Organosis Kyprion Agoniston, or the National Organisation of Cypriot Fighters) begins a guerilla campaign to unite Cyprus with Greece.

1960 Cyprus granted independence. Archbishop Makarios III becomes president.

1963 Inter-communal fighting. Turks retreat into enclaves.

1974 Military coup. Makarios flees the island. Turkish forces invade and control northern Cyprus. Makarios returns.

1983 Turks unilaterally proclaim the 'Turkish Republic of Northern Cyprus'.

2003 Greek and Turkish Cypriots cross the Green Line—for the first time in nearly 30 years.

2004 A UN reunification referendum gets Turkish-Cypriot support, but overwhelming Greek-Cypriot rejection. Greek Cyprus joins the European Union.

2008 In a symbolic gesture, Turkish Cypriot leader Mehmet Ali Talat crosses the Green Line at the new Ledra Street checkpoint in Nicosia.

ARCHBISHOP MAKARIOS III

Mikhail Khristodolou Mouskos (1913–77) was the leader in the struggle for *enosis* (union) with Greece. This son of a shepherd gained support from Greece to pursue independence from the British, landing him in exile in 1956. The EOKA (the armed nationalist movement) intensified its campaign and Makarios returned to Cyprus to become the first president in 1960 with only a coup in 1974 interrupting his presidency until his death 1977

CYPRUS FOR SALE

When Richard the Lionheart dropped in on Limassol during a storm, he also took the island by storm and then sold it to the Knights Templar. When the Knights couldn't raise the asking price, Richard sold it on to Guy of Lusignan for a handsome sum.

Index

INDEX

127

TWINPACK
Cyprus

WRITTEN BY Lara Dunston
VERIFIED BY George McDonald and Lindsay Bennett
COVER DESIGN AND DESIGN WORK Jacqueline Bailey
INDEXER Marie Lorimer
IMAGE RETOUCHING AND REPRO Sarah Montgomery, Michael Moody and James Tims
PROJECT EDITOR Apostrophe S Limited
SERIES EDITOR Cathy Harrison

© **AA MEDIA LIMITED 2010**

Colour separation by AA Digital Department
Printed and bound by Leo Paper Products, China

A CIP catalogue record for this book is available from the British Library.

ISBN 978-0-7495-6150-5

Published by AA Publishing, a trading name of AA Media Limited, whose registered office is Fanum House, Basing View, Basingstoke, Hampshire RG21 4EA. Registered number 06112600.

At the time of writing the UK does not recognize the self-declared Turkish Republic of Northern Cyprus (TRNC). For updated information on developments refer to the British Foreign Office website at www.fco.gov.uk.

Front cover image: AA/S Day
Back cover images: (i) and (iv) AA/S Day; (ii) AA/C Sawyer; (iii) AA/A Kouprianoff

A03639
Maps in this title produced from mapping © Freytag-Berndt u. Artaria KG, 1231 Vienna-Austria with additional information from Cyprus Tourism Organisation © State Copyright reserved and Turkish Republic of Northern Cyprus tourist office

The Automobile Association would like to thank the following photographers, companies and picture libraries for their assistance in the preparation of this book.

Abbreviations for the pictures credits are as follows – (t) top; (b) bottom; (c) centre; (l) left; (r) right; (AA) AA World Travel Library.

1 AA/A Kouprianoff; 2–18 top panel AA/M Birkitt; 4 AA/S Day; 5 AA/A Kouprianoff; 6tl AA/A Kouprianoff; 6tc AA/M Birkitt; 6tr AA/M Birkitt; 6bl AA/C Sawyer; 6bc AA/A Kouprianoff; 6br AA/A Kouprianoff; 7tl AA/T Harris; 7tc AA/S Day; 7tr AA/A Kouprianoff; 7bl AA/M Birkitt; 7bc AA/A Kouprianoff; 7br AA/A Kouprianoff; 10t AA/H Ulucam; 10c(i) AA/M Birkitt; 10c(ii) AA/S Day; 10b AA/M Birkitt; 11t(i) AA/A Kouprianoff; 11t(ii) AA/R Rainford; 11c(i) AA/M Birkitt; 11c(ii) AA/S Day; 11b AA/S Day; 12t AA/A Kouprianoff; 12c(i) AA/A Kouprianoff; 12c(ii) AA/A Kouprianoff; 12b AA/A Kouprianoff; 13t(i) AA; 13t(ii) AA/C Sawyer; 13c(i) AA/J Tims; 13c(ii) AA/C Sawyer; 13b AA/M Birkitt; 14t AA/A Kouprianoff; 14c(i) AA/M Birkitt; 14c(ii) AA/K Paterson; 14b AA/A Kouprianoff; 15 AA/C Sawyer; 16t AA/H Ulucam; 16c(i) AA/A Kouprianoff; 16c(ii) AA/A Kouprianoff; 16b AA/R Rainford; 17t AA/M Birkitt; 17c(i) AA/R Rainford; 17c(ii) AA/A Kouprianoff; 17b AA/A Kouprianoff; 18t AA/J Holmes; 18c(i) The Londa Hotel; 18c(ii) Ingram; 18b AA/M Birkitt; 19t(i) AA/M Birkitt; 19t(ii) AA/M Birkitt; 19c(i) AA/A Kouprianoff; 19c(ii) AA/A Kouprianoff; 19b AA/H Ulucam; 20–21 AA/M Birkitt; 24l AA/M Birkitt; 24c AA/S Day; 24r AA/A Kouprianoff; 25l AA/M Birkitt; 25c AA/M Birkitt; 25r AA/R Rainford; 26–27 top panel AA/R Rainford; 26l AA/M Birkitt; 26r AA/A Kouprianoff; 27l AA/A Kouprianoff; 27r AA/S Day; 28 AA/H Ulucam; 29 AA/M Birkitt; 30 AA/C Sawyer; 31 AA/M Birkitt; 34l AA/M Birkitt; 34r AA/S Day; 35 AA/A Kouprianoff; 36l AA/A Kouprianoff; 36c AA/A Kouprianoff; 37l AA/R Rainford; 37c AA/M Birkitt; 37r AA/A Kouprianoff; 38l Photolibrary; 38r AA/M Birkitt; 39l AA/S Day; 39r AA/M Birkitt; 40–41 top panel AA/S Day; 40l AA/S Day; 40r AA/A Kouprianoff; 41l AA/M Birkitt; 41r AA/M Birkitt; 42 AA/A Kouprianoff; 43 AA/M Birkitt; 44 AA/H Ulucam; 45 AA/M Birkitt; 46 AA/C Sawyer; 47 AA/S Day; 50l AA/S Day; 50r AA/S Day; 51 AA/S Day; 52l AA/M Birkitt; 52r AA/A Kouprianoff; 53l AA/A Kouprianoff; 53c AA/S Day; 53r AA/M Birkitt; 54 AA/S Day, 55l AA/R Rainford, 55bl AA/A Kouprianoff; 55br AA/A Kouprianoff; 56 top panel AA/A Kouprianoff; 56b AA/S Day; 57 AA/A Kouprianoff; 58l AA/S Day; 58r AA/S Day; 59l AA/M Birkitt; 59r AA/A Kouprianoff; 60 AA/S Day; 61 AA/H Ulucam; 62 AA/M Birkitt; 63 AA/A Kouprianoff; 64 AA/C Sawyer; 65 AA/S Day; 68l AA/M Birkitt; 68c AA/A Kouprianoff; 68r AA/R Rainford; 69l AA/S Day; 69c AA/S Day; 69r AA/A Kouprianoff; 70l AA/A Kouprianoff; 70r AA/A Kouprianoff; 71l AA/M Birkitt; 71c AA/R Rainford; 71r AA/R Rainford; 72l AA/S Day; 72c AA/R Rainford; 72r AA/S Day; 73–77 top panel AA/S Day; 73b AA/A Kouprianoff; 74l AA/A Kouprianoff; 74r AA/M Birkitt; 75 AA/M Birkitt; 76l AA/A Kouprianoff; 76r AA/A Kouprianoff; 77l AA/M Birkitt; 77r AA/A Kouprianoff; 78 AA/R Bulmar; 79–80 AA/H Ulucam; 81–82 AA/M Birkitt; 83–84 AA/C Sawyer; 85 AA/A Kouprianoff; 88l AA/A Kouprianoff; 88r AA/A Kouprianoff; 89 AA/A Kouprianoff; 90l AA/A Kouprianoff; 90r AA/A Kouprianoff; 91t AA/H Ulucam; 91bl AA/R Bulmar; 91br AA/A Kouprianoff; 92l AA/A Kouprianoff; 92c AA/A Kouprianoff; 92r Imagebroker/Alamy; 93l AA/R Bulmar; 93r AA/A Kouprianoff; 94l AA; 94/95t AA/A Kouprianoff; 94bl AA/A Kouprianoff; 65bl AA/A Kouprianoff; 95r AA/A Kouprianoff; 96l AA/A Kouprianoff; 96c AA/A Kouprianoff; 96r AA/A Kouprianoff; 97l AA/M Birkitt; 97c AA/A Kouprianoff; 97r AA/A Kouprianoff; 98l AA/A Kouprianoff; 98c AA/A Kouprianoff; 98r AA/R Bulmar; 99l AA/A Kouprianoff; 99r AA/A Kouprianoff; 100–101 top panel AA/A Kouprianoff; 100l AA/A Kouprianoff; 100r AA/A Kouprianoff; 101l AA/M Birkitt; 101r AA/A Kouprianoff; 102 AA/A Kouprianoff; 103 AA/H Ulucam; 104 AA/M Birkitt; 105–106 AA/C Sawyer; 107 AA/A Kouprianoff; 108–109 top panel AA/C Sawyer; 108t AA/A Kouprianoff; 108c(i) AA/M Birkitt; 108c(ii) AA/A Kouprianoff; 108b AA/A Kouprianoff; 113 AA/M Birkitt; 114–125 top panel AA/R Rainford; 120 AA/M Lynch; 121 AA/S Day; 122 AA/C Sawyer; 123 AA/A Kouprianoff; 124l AA/A Kouprianoff; 124c AA/R Rainford; 124r AA/A Kouprianoff; 125l AA/M Birkitt; 125c AA/M Birkitt; 125r AA/M Birkitt.

Every effort has been made to trace the copyright holders, and we apologise in advance for any accidental errors. We would be happy to apply any corrections in the following edition of this publication.